OECD ECONOMIC SURVEYS

AUSTRIA

FEBRUARY 1985

ORGANISATION FOR ECONOMIC CO-OPERATION AND DEVELOPMENT

Pursuant to article 1 of the Convention signed in Paris on 14th December, 1960, and which came into force on 30th September, 1961, the Organisation for Economic Co-operation and Development (OECD) shall promote policies designed:

- to achieve the highest sustainable economic growth and employment and a rising standard of living in Member countries, while maintaining financial stability, and thus to contribute to the development of the world economy;
- to contribute to sound economic expansion in Member as well as non-member countries in the process of economic development; and
- to contribute to the expansion of world trade on a multilateral, non-discriminatory basis in accordance with international obligations.

The Signatories of the Convention on the OECD are Austria, Belgium, Canada, Denmark, France, the Federal Republic of Germany, Greece, Iceland, Ireland, Italy, Luxembourg, the Netherlands, Norway, Portugal, Spain, Sweden, Switzerland, Turkey, the United Kingdom and the United States. The following countries acceded subsequently to this Convention (the dates are those on which the instruments of accession were deposited): Japan (28th April, 1964), Finland (28th January, 1969), Australia (7th June, 1971) and New Zealand (29th May, 1973).

The Socialist Federal Republic of Yugoslavia takes part in certain work of the OECD (agreement of 28th October, 1961).

CONTENTS

I.   Introduction: the current upswing and policy problems   7

II. Main features of developments in 1983-84   9
     Demand and output   9
     The labour market   13
     Prices, wages and profits   16
     Balance of payments   19

III. Macroeconomic policies and short-term prospects   23
     Fiscal policy   23
     Monetary policy, money and credit   28
     Short-term prospects   33

IV. Some aspects of structural adjustment in industry   36

V.   Conclusions   48

Notes and references   50

Annexes:
     I.   Supporting material on structural change in industry   52
     II. Calendar of main economic events   56

Statistical annex   60

TABLES

Text

1. Demand and output   10
2. Labour market developments   14
3. Incomes, costs and prices   17
4. Exchange rate developments and international competitiveness   21
5. Balance of payments: recent trends   22
6. The Federal Budget   24
7. Fiscal policy indicators   26
8. Monetary developments   32
9. Financial balances   33

3

10.	Short-term prospects	35
11.	Manufacturing sector's performance in international comparison	37
12.	The composition of manufacturing output	38
13.	Share of high technology products in exports and imports of manufactures	41
14.	Subsidisation by General Government	47

Annexes

A1.	Relative performance of the manufacturing sector	52
A2.	Foundations and closures of establishments in industry	53
A3.	Cash flow as a per cent of gross earnings in industry	53
A4.	Real gross fixed capital formation in manufacturing industry	54
A5.	State-owned industries' relative economic performance	54

Statistical annex

A.	Gross domestic product	60
B.	General government income and expenditure	61
C.	Output, employment, wages and productivity in industry	62
D.	Retail sales and prices	63
E.	Money and banking	64
F.	The Federal budget	65
G.	Balance of payments	66
H.	Merchandise trade by commodity group and area	68

DIAGRAMS

Text

1.	Economic performance indicators	8
2.	Cyclical comparison of demand components	11
3.	Cyclical comparison of output, employment and prices	12
4.	The labour market	15
5.	Factor incomes and shares	18
6.	Balance of payments developments	20
7.	Government debt	27
8.	Interest rates	30
9.	Monetary indicators	31
10.	Leading indicators	34
11.	The output structure in international comparison	40
12.	International comparison of cash-flow and own capital ratios	43
13.	Profits and investment in the manufacturing sector	44

Annex

A1.	Profit indicators	55

4

BASIC STATISTICS OF AUSTRIA

THE LAND

Area (thousand km²)	84	Major cities, 1981 census (thousands of inhabitants):
Agricultural area (thousand km²), 1980	37	Vienna 1 531
Exploited forest area (thousand km²)	32	Graz 243
		Linz 200
		Salzburg 139
		Innsbruck 117

THE PEOPLE

Population, 31.12.83 (thousands)	7 551	Net migration, 1983	−1 900
per km²	90	Total employment[1], monthly average 1983	2 734 700
Net natural increase in population, 1983	−2 923	of which:	
Natural increase rate per 1 000 inhabitants, 1983	−0.4	in industry[2]	567 400

PRODUCTION

Gross Domestic Product, 1983 (Sch. billion)	1 206	Industrial origin of GDP at market prices, 1983 (per cent):	
per head (US $)	8 888	Agriculture	4
Gross fixed investment, average 1981-1983:		Industry	27
per cent of GDP	23	Construction	7
per head (US $)	2 075	Other	62

THE GOVERNMENT

Public consumption, 1983 (per cent of GDP)	19	Composition of Federal Parliament, April 1983:	
General government current revenue, 1983		Socialist Party	90
(per cent of GDP)	47	Austrian People's Party	81
Federal Government debt, end 1983 (per cent of GDP)	35	Liberal Party	12
		Last election: 1983	
		Next election: 1987	

FOREIGN TRADE

Exports:		Imports:	
Exports of goods and services, 1981-1983		Imports of goods and services, 1981-1983	
(per cent of GDP) average	41	(per cent of GDP) average	41
Exports, 1983 (per cent of total merchandise exports):		Imports, 1983 (per cent of total merchandise imports):	
Food, tobacco, beverages	4	Food, tobacco, beverages	6
Raw materials and energy	8	Raw materials and energy	20
Chemicals	9	Chemicals	10
Machinery and transport equipment	30	Machinery and transport equipment	30
Other finished and semi-manufactured products	48	Other finished and semi-manufactured products	34

THE CURRENCY

Monetary unit: Schilling	Currency units per US dollar, average of daily figures:	
	Year 1984	20.01
	December 1984	21.76

1. Wage and salary earners.
2. Including administrative personnel.
Note: An international comparison of certain basic statistics is given in an annex table.

5

I. INTRODUCTION:
THE CURRENT UPSWING AND POLICY PROBLEMS

In various respects the present economic upswing in Austria compares favourably with that of many other OECD countries (Diagram 1). Real GDP growth, a little over 2 per cent per annum between 1982 and 1984, has been above the European OECD average. The unemployment rate, at about 4 per cent of the total labour force, is among the lowest in the OECD area. Inflation, despite the recent rise, is still about 2½ percentage points below the average for European Member countries. And the external balance, although deteriorating, is broadly in equilibrium. Satisfactory macroeconomic performance is also expected over the next eighteen months: a continuation of the economic recovery, low inflation, a slight improvement in labour market conditions and a broadly unchanged external payments position (see Part III). But these developments contain certain elements of weakness which could present the authorities with medium-term policy problems.

Compared with the previous recovery phase of the mid-1970s, the present growth of real GDP does appear slower and the unemployment rate substantially higher (Diagram 1). The weaker expansion of output in the present upswing is attributable to slower growth of world trade (5½ per cent from 1982 to 1984 compared with 8½ per cent from 1975 to 1977 at annual rates) and a smaller demand impact of policy. In 1975-76 the expansionary *ex ante* swing of fiscal balance amounted to nearly 5 per cent of GDP, fiscal support continuing strongly into the second year of the upswing. But the discretionary budget change towards expansion in 1982-83 was a modest 1¼ per cent of GDP, the fiscal policy stance having been turned towards restriction in 1984, the second year of the upturn. The monetary policy stance was eased prior to the upturn of activity in both cases but appears to be tighter in the present recovery as indicated by high real interest rates.

The reason for the more prudent fiscal policy in the current upswing is the strongly rising public debt and servicing costs which have diminished the scope for fiscal support to activity (see Part III). After a tightening until 1981, the fiscal policy stance shifted towards expansion in 1982-83 in contrast to policies in many other countries. It was tightened again in 1984 but will apparently be broadly neutral in 1985. Unless the budget deficit is reduced substantially, the rise in public debt cannot be contained and the room for manoeuvre for fiscal policy can only be narrowed further.

Inflationary pressure was reduced sharply in the course of both the previous and present recoveries, helped by low import price increases. But, despite the adverse effects of tax increases, inflation has been lower than in the mid-1970s as unit labour cost increases were more moderate. Wage moderation contributed. But an important feature this time was that the productivity increase resulted from a substantial labour shake-out, which was probably inevitable given the weakness of activity, but represented a departure from past attitudes of firms to maintain the workforce through the recession. As a consequence, labour market conditions deteriorated substantially in the 1980s. Although the unemployment rate is stabilising, the structure of unemployment with an increasing share of young adults and long-time unemployed is a matter of concern (see labour market section in Part II).

Diagram 1. Economic performance indicators

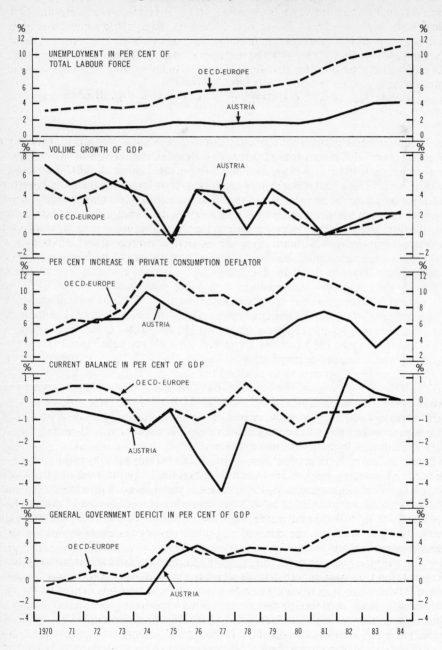

Sources: WIFO; National Bank; Ministry of Finance; OECD Secretariat.

The level of interest rates in the current upturn could have been lower but for the exchange rate link to the Deutschemark (see Part III). Lower interest rates presumably would have had some positive effects on activity. Moreover, wage settlements could present a problem if they result in a deterioration in competitiveness vis-à-vis Germany in the medium term (see inflation section of Part II). The real appreciation of the currency during the 1970s probably worked as a catalyst for structural change in industry. But, given the weakening of structural adaptation in industry since the mid-1970s (see Part IV), a renewed real appreciation of the schilling may become an important policy problem over the medium term.

Finally, as featured in Part IV, structural change in industry, despite a move towards a higher share of technology-intensive products, has slowed since the mid-1970s, and gaps vis-à-vis high-income industrial nations still remain in terms of either the level of productivity or the production structure. Among the possible factors behind these developments are relatively low research-and-development expenditure, insufficient supply of risk capital and the priority of policy placed on the maintenance of employment levels until recently. Although the policy orientation has since shifted towards fostering structural adjustment, the existing system of subsidisation, which is under review, does not always seem to be well suited to facilitate structural changes. Structurally-weak industries, where nationalised companies are mainly operating, are faced with a difficult task of adjustment which has obvious implications for employment.

II. MAIN FEATURES OF DEVELOPMENTS IN 1983-84

Demand and output

After nearly stagnating during 1982, real GDP picked up in 1983, expanding strongly through the year (Table 1). The recovery was led by private consumption and stockbuilding, investment picking up only later in the year. Although foreign demand revived too in the course of 1983, the growth contribution of the real foreign balance turned strongly negative due to buoyant import demand. The economic upturn continued in 1984 despite the budget consolidation measures which affected both the time profile and the pace of the recovery. Because of imminent tax increases, purchases were brought forward into 1983 and domestic demand declined in the first half of 1984. A positive growth contribution of the real foreign balance, however, led to a slight increase in real GDP. Although import growth continued to be strong due to a shift in the demand structure towards equipment investment and stockbuilding (components with a high import content) this was outweighed by export growth which was accelerating further (both import and export growth rates in Table 1 are, however, biased upwards as they include transit trade which has risen sharply over the last year; see the Balance of Payments section below). The rise in real net exports seems to have gone on in the second half of the year, with foreign demand unabated but import growth slowing somewhat, reflecting decelerating restocking. Machinery and equipment investment, too, has apparently kept growing, after a temporary weakening in mid-1984. Although construction investment and consumer demand were sluggish up to the summer, they are likely to have stopped falling in the second half of the year. The resulting pick-up of domestic demand seems to have been sufficient to lead to a marked acceleration of real GDP growth. Hence the expansion of real GDP in 1984 as a whole would seem to have been much the same as in the previous year.

Table 1. Demand and output

	Per cent of GDP at current prices 1982	1982	1983	1984 I / 1983 I	1983 I	1983 II	1984 I	1984 Q1	1984 Q2	1984 Q3
Private consumption	56.5	1.4	5.0	-0.1	8.4	3.5	-3.7	-10.0	-1.0	4.1
Government consumption	18.8	2.3	2.0	2.0	1.6	1.7	2.3	2.8	1.5	1.4
Gross fixed capital formation	23.1	-6.8	-1.9	3.3	-3.2	5.4	1.3	-5.7	9.7	-11.7
Construction	13.4	6.4	-0.8	-0.0	-4.2	8.5	-7.9	-17.0	-6.8	4.7
Machinery and equipment	9.7	-7.2	-3.2	7.3	-2.0	1.7	13.2	9.9	31.7	-27.1
Final domestic demand	98.4	-0.4	2.8	1.0	4.4	3.6	-1.4	-6.7	1.8	-0.2
Stockbuilding[1,2]	-0.1	-0.5	0.6	1.8	0.4	2.5	1.0	0.2	-1.1	5.4
Total domestic demand	98.3	-0.9	3.5	2.9	4.9	6.2	-0.4	-6.5	0.6	5.3
Foreign balance[1]	1.7	1.9	-1.2	-0.2	-2.8	-1.5	1.1	6.8	-3.5	-1.3
Exports of goods and services	40.7	2.1	6.2	19.0	7.2	16.7	21.3	25.8	28.7	14.8
Imports of goods and services	39.1	-2.6	9.9	20.7	15.6	22.0	19.5	9.1	40.4	18.2
GDP	100.0	1.0	2.1	2.6	1.8	4.5	0.7	0.2	-2.9	3.9
Memorandum items:										
GDP deflator		6.7	3.7	4.4	3.2	3.8	5.1	5.8	1.9	3.2
Industrial production		-0.8	0.9	5.0	2.1	5.8	4.2	8.9	1.9	11.8

1. Changes in stockbuilding and the foreign balance are expressed in per cent of GDP of the previous period, at annual rates.
2. Including statistical discrepancy.
Sources: WIFO, OECD Secretariat.

10

A revival of private consumption at the turn of 1983, prompted by falling inflation and interest rates as well as pent-up demand, could be observed in many countries but was particularly strong in Austria due to the stance of fiscal policy and some special factors. While in other countries the drop in the inflation rate just sufficed to stop the fall in real incomes, in Austria the rise in real disposable income of households accelerated to more than 3 per cent,

Diagram 2. **Cyclical comparison of demand components**
Constant prices; seasonally adjusted

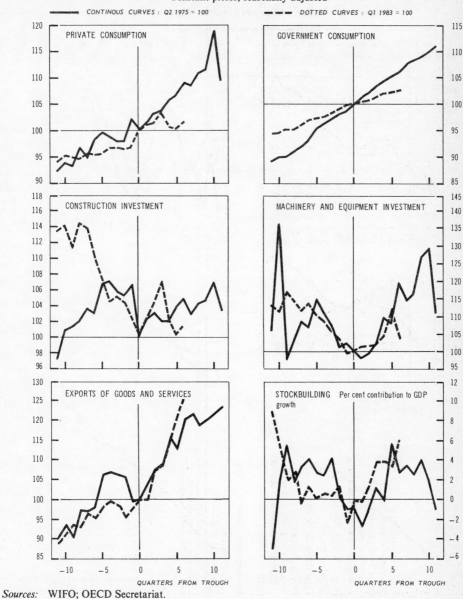

Sources: WIFO; OECD Secretariat.

helped by the second stage of income tax cuts and a relatively strong expansion of social transfers. With expectations of tax increases also boosting consumer demand in the course of 1983, its real expansion exceeded that of household incomes by almost 2 percentage points. As a consequence of VAT-related pre-buying, in particular of durables, some upward adjustment of the saving ratio would have been expected in early 1984. The rise in the saving ratio in 1984, however, seems to have been sizeable. Increasing inflation and interest rates

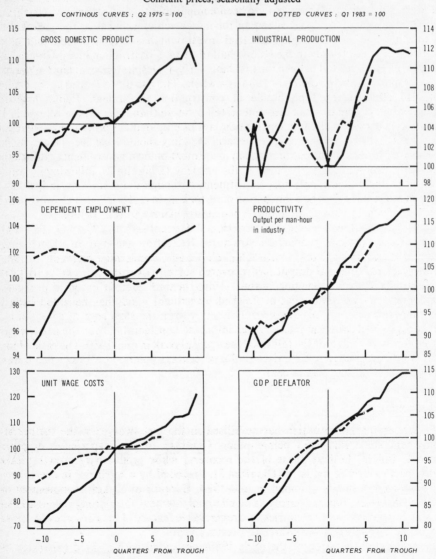

Diagram 3. **Cyclical comparison of output, employment and prices**

Constant prices; seasonally adjusted

Sources: WIFO; OECD Secretariat.

12

may have played a role. The fall in real private consumption, at about 1 per cent, nevertheless, is likely to have been smaller than projected as household incomes developed better than expected. The downward trend of employment having been reversed, growth of disposable income of households seems to have accelerated somewhat in 1984, to give a slight increase in real terms, in spite of the marked rise in the inflation rate. Nevertheless, real income growth, and hence growth of real consumer demand, have been much lower in the current cycle than in the 1970s. The same is true for government consumption, although its rate of expansion was kept broadly stable during the recession (Diagram 2).

Gross fixed capital formation recovered through 1983 but still fell in the year as a whole (Table 1). The expansion of machinery and equipment investment accelerated markedly in 1984, the pace of recovery having so far been comparable to past experience (Diagram 2). Initially reflecting mainly higher spending for motor vehicles, it has in the meantime also spread to other equipment items. Industrial investment has lagged behind that of other sectors, reviving strongly only in the second half of 1984. Construction investment picked up in the course of 1983 but fell back in the first half of 1984. Despite a revival later in the year, it may have dropped again in volume in 1984 as a whole. The rise in VAT rates at the beginning of 1984 also affected the time profile of construction investment. Public investment, consisting mainly of construction investment, fell by more than 5 per cent in volume in 1983, the fifth drop in a row, as the implementation lags of employment programmes were longer than expected. In 1984, however, higher Federal spending should have been largely sufficient to compensate for the continuing decrease in investment of local governments. Stockbuilding was unusually strong in the early phase of the upswing (Diagram 2), following a protracted period of weak demand and inventory adjustment. Although there are some indications of a slowdown in recent months, the contribution of restocking in real GDP growth is likely to have more than doubled in 1984 from about ½ percentage point the year before.

Overall output growth of slightly more than 2 per cent in both 1983 and 1984 conceals important changes in the production structure. Reflecting the pattern of demand, the expansion of the service sector, in particular retail trade, accelerated markedly in 1983 but slowed thereafter. Industrial output has recovered steadily over the last two years (Table 1 and Diagram 3) with construction output falling behind. Output of basic products has expanded most rapidly while that of finished investment goods has benefited little from buoyant domestic demand, picking up only lately. Given the slow pace of potential output growth, capacity utilisation in industry has improved considerably over the past two years, making up for more than half the fall since the cyclical peak in mid-1980. The ratio of total to potential GDP is estimated to have risen by 1½ percentage points since 1982 when it was at a historical low of less than 95 per cent.

The labour market

The labour market situation has stabilised in the last two years, the further rise in unemployment since mid-1983 being minor. Contrary to past experience, employment continued to fall in the first phase of the recovery, while productivity growth picked up markedly, particularly in industry (Diagram 3). Preceded by a rapid rise in overtime work, employment growth finally resumed in mid-1984. Because of a parallel movement of the labour force, however, this has hardly affected unemployment. The strong rebound in labour supply, also observed in other countries, is a remarkable feature of the current cycle, reversing the rise in the discouraged work-force in previous years.

The protracted recession of the early 1980s coincided with a rapid expansion of the potential labour force for demographic reasons. But with labour market conditions

13

Table 2. **Labour market developments**

	1978	1979	1980	1981	1982	1983	1984
	Percentage changes						
Population of working age	1.1	1.1	0.9	0.8	0.9	0.4	0.6
Total labour force							
Mikrozensus[4]	1.3	1.2	0.4	1.3	0.1	−0.3	0.3[5]
WIFO	0.5	0.1	0.1	0.6	−0.1	−0.5	0.2
Total employment							
Mikrozensus[4]	0.9	1.2	0.6	0.7	−1.0	−1.0	0.2[5]
WIFO	0.2	0.2	0.2	0.1	−1.2	−1.2	0.1
National accounts	0.3	0.4	1.0	−0.3	−1.4	−0.8	
Dependent employment[1]	0.7	1.0	0.7	0.4	−1.4	−0.8	0.4
Industry	−1.7	−0.1	1.1	−2.1	−4.0	−4.0	−1.0[5]
Foreign workers	−6.4	−3.5	2.4	−1.7	−9.2	−7.0	−4.6
	Levels (thousands)						
Unemployed							
Mikrozensus	64	65	58	80	115	135	139[5]
Registered	59	57	53	69	105	127	130
Unfilled vacancies	29	31	36	25	17	15	17
	Per cent						
Unemployment rate							
Mikrozensus[2,4]	2.0	2.0	1.8	2.4	3.4	4.1	4.2[5]
Registered[3]	2.1	2.0	1.9	2.4	3.7	4.5	4.5
Vacancies/unemployed							
Mikrozensus	45.3	47.7	62.1	31.3	14.8	11.1	12.2[5]
Registered	49.2	54.4	67.9	36.2	16.2	11.8	13.0

1. Social security statistics adjusted by WIFO.
2. Per cent of total labour force.
3. Per cent of dependent labour force.
4. Adjusted by the Secretariat for break in the series in 1981/82 and 1983/84.
5. Secretariat estimate.
Sources: Austrian Central Statistical Office (Mikrozensus); Ministry of Social Affairs; WIFO; OECD Secretariat.

deteriorating markedly, the actual labour force stagnated in 1982 and even dropped in 1983 (Table 2). This was in part attributable to sizeable net emigration which reduced the working age population by almost 1 per cent in 1982-83. In addition, a rise in the discouraged work-force, as estimated on the basis of demographic and participation rate trends, cut down the labour force. Early retirement also increased significantly. Labour force participation fell from 70½ per cent in the early 1980s to 68½ per cent in 1983, despite an ongoing rise in the middle age brackets of women. The decline in participation rates was most pronounced in the lowest and highest age groups. Between 1980 and 1983, labour force participation of people from 60 to 65 years decreased by 7½ percentage points to 15 per cent (males: 12½ points to 22 per cent). Early retirement has doubled since the late 1970s to about 3 per cent of the actual labour force. In 1984, both the growth of early retirement and the rise in the discouraged work-force seem to have slowed somewhat. As net emigration also decelerated, growth of labour supply resumed but still remained markedly below that of the potential labour force (as calculated on the basis of participation rate trends, and excluding net emigration).

With real GDP growth accelerating only little, the slight rise in employment in 1984, after the marked fall in the year before (Table 2), mainly reflected a slowdown of productivity

Diagram 4. The labour market

Seasonally adjusted quarterly data

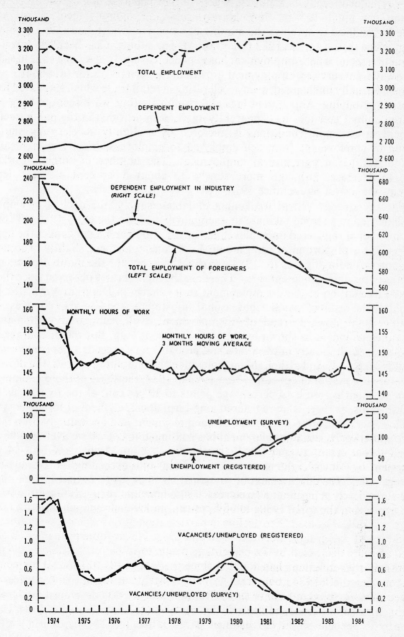

Sources: WIFO; Austrian Central Statistical Office; OECD Secretariat.

15

growth from 3 to 2 per cent. On an hourly basis, the latter decelerated even more, as average working time increased in 1984 following a slight drop in 1983. However, cyclical productivity gains have remained strong in industry, where output per man-hour grew by 6½ per cent in 1983 and not much less in 1984. Nevertheless, the vigorous recovery of industrial production has sufficed to stabilise the number of employees which had fallen by more than 10 per cent in the three years to 1983 (Diagram 4). The situation has been less favourable in the construction sector where employment has kept decreasing. In spite of a shift in the output structure away from services, employment growth in the tertiary sector (at about 1 per cent) has remained virtually unchanged, even accelerating in retail trade which stagnated following VAT-related pre-buying. Adjustment lags and rising part-time work seem to have played a role. But the bulk of new jobs has apparently again been provided in the public sector. The improvement in economic conditions is mirrored by a slightly accelerating shift in the composition of employment from self-employed to employees, mainly as a result of an accentuated decline in agricultural employment. The number of foreign workers has continued to decrease, although more slowly, to about 5 per cent of total dependent employment, the lowest figure since 1970.

Despite the strong cyclical weakening of labour supply, the decline in employment in 1982-83 has led to a strong increase in unemployment since the early 1980s (Table 2). In 1983, the number of registered unemployed reached 127 000 or 4.5 per cent of the dependent labour force. As a proportion of total labour force, unemployment slightly exceeded 4 per cent. The corresponding figures for 1984 are slightly higher for the number of unemployed and unchanged for unemployment rates. These are the highest rates observed since the 1950s. The marked fluctuation of the unemployment series shown in Diagram 4 over the last two years is mainly the result of insufficient seasonal adjustment. Year-on-year changes suggest a fairly stable slight upward trend of unemployment. Still, compared with many other countries, unemployment as shown by the statistics is not high. But the discouraged labour force has grown substantially in the 1980s and probably now exceeds 1 per cent even if early retirement is excluded. And although unemployment has stabilised overall, the development of its structure is a matter of concern. From 1983 to 1984, the share of those unemployed for more than six months rose by 4 percentage points to 30 per cent of the total. This figure is biased downwards, as there is no registered long-term unemployment of foreigners (they are not eligible for benefits after six months of unemployment and accordingly drop out of the statistics). Moreover, youth unemployment has continued to rise above average, the share of people below the age of twenty-five in the total reaching 31 per cent in 1984 and the unemployment rate of the eighteen to twenty-five year-olds exceeding the average by about 1 percentage point. The development of participation rates suggests that hidden unemployment of young people, in particular foreigners, is also high and rising, as first-time job seekers partly escape registration, not being eligible for unemployment compensation.

Prices, wages and profits

Consumer price inflation came down to 3.3 per cent in 1983, the lowest figure in fifteen years and among the lowest in the OECD area. The fall in world market prices for raw materials and energy products contributed. But unit labour costs developed favourably, too, even falling in industry (Table 3). The inflation performance deteriorated in 1984. Consumer prices rose by 5¾ per cent, slightly exceeding the OECD average. The increase in VAT rates at the beginning of the year seems to have been almost fully passed through, probably adding about 2 per cent to consumer prices. Import prices also started rising again, mostly due to the higher U.S. dollar. But unit labour cost increases remained modest so that, taking account of

16

Table 3. **Incomes, costs and prices**

Table 3. **Incomes, costs and prices**

	1978	1979	1980	1981	1982	1983	1984
	Percentage changes						
Wages and salaries							
Contractual wages							
Total economy, per head	7.0	5.1	5.4	7.2	7.2	5.1	4.3
Industry, workers per hour	5.9	5.4	6.1	7.0	7.4	5.6	4.4
Effective earnings							
Total economy, per head	7.0	5.5	6.2	7.9	5.7	4.9	5.1
Industry, workers, per hour[1]	5.6	6.0	6.3	7.2	3.9	4.9	3.9
Disposable income							
Employees and pensioners	7.2	7.2	6.8	7.0	6.2	4.9	5.2
Households	6.5	9.2	6.2	5.3	8.9	6.5	6.8
Unit factor cost							
Unit wage cost							
Total economy	9.0	2.0	5.0	8.4	3.4	2.1	3.2
Industry	2.7	−0.5	4.7	7.7	2.9	−0.5	−0.7
Gross profit margins	−0.8	11.8	8.1	−0.7	18.3	7.1	7.0
Prices							
GDP deflator	5.2	4.1	5.4	6.3	6.6	3.7	4.4
Consumption deflator	4.3	4.5	6.5	7.5	6.4	3.2	5.7
Consumer price index	3.6	3.7	6.4	6.8	5.4	3.3	5.6
Wholesale price index[2]	1.0	4.2	8.6	8.1	3.1	0.6	3.8
Construction prices							
Residential construction	6	5	8	8	6	3	3
Road building	9	15	17	9	4	0	−1
Foreign trade prices							
Merchandise exports	0.0	4.1	5.0	6.1	4.5	−0.3	4.0
Merchandise imports	−0.1	5.5	10.6	10.5	0.4	−1.2	4.5
	Per cent						
Memorandum items:							
Wage share in national income	75.7	74.0	74.0	75.9	73.7	72.7	72.3
Adjusted for changes in the employment structure since 1970	69.5	67.6	67.3	68.9	66.9	66.0	65.5

1. Excluding vacation bonuses.
2. Excluding VAT.
Sources: Austrian Central Statistical Office; WIFO; OECD Secretariat.

the VAT increase, inflationary pressures do not appear to have risen much in 1984. Reflecting depressed prices in the construction sector and deteriorating terms of trade, the growth rate of the GDP deflator is estimated to have accelerated by only 1 percentage point to 4½ per cent in 1984.

Modest cost pressure and demand recovery allowed a continuing restoration of profit margins in 1984. Manufacturing profitability improved strongly, in particular in the export sector, as unit labour costs kept falling while export prices increased almost equally with import prices (Table 3). The cash-flow/gross earnings ratio of industrial corporations improved from 18½ per cent in 1981 to about 25 per cent in 1984, about the 1976 level but still significantly below the level of the first half of the 1970s (Annex Table 3). The rising cash-flow has so far financed most of capital spending by business. The share of the operating surplus in national income rose from a trough of 24 per cent in 1981 to almost 28 per cent in 1984. Adjusted for changes in the composition of employment from self-employed to employees, the functional income distribution is now back at about the 1973-74 level (Diagram 5).

Diagram 5. **Factor incomes and shares**

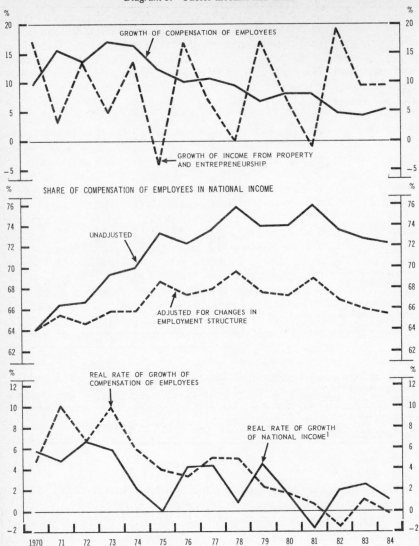

1. Adjusted for changes in the terms of trade.
Sources: Austrian Central Statistical Office; OECD Secretariat.

Wage developments are largely determined by collective agreements, negotiated and concluded in annual wage rounds, starting usually in autumn and stretching out into the following year. The 1983-84 pay round was still under the influence of the continuing rise in unemployment and marked falls in the inflation rate in the initial stage of the recovery. Nevertheless, its outcome represented a departure from past attitudes as trade unions accepted an *ex ante* fall in real wages, abstaining from requesting compensation for the inflationary impact of budget consolidation measures (inflation was expected to rise to 5 per cent in 1984). The pace was set as usual by the metal workers with minimum and effective (for employees who are paid more than minimum rates) wage increases of 3½ and 3 per cent, respectively. Wage settlements were not much higher in other sectors less exposed to international competition. Generally they provided for minimum and effective wage increases which were respectively 2½ and 1½ per cent below those of the preceding year. Reflecting these settlements and partly already those of the current pay round, basic wages grew by 4½ per cent in 1984, ½ percentage point less than in 1983, with the deceleration more pronounced in industry (Table 3). Wagedrift increased slightly due mainly to overtime work. Excluding these effects, wagedrift may still have been negative, in particular in industry. Growth of gross effective earnings per employee – including wagedrift – remained practically unchanged at 5 per cent. Given the acceleration of inflation, however, this implies a drop in real terms. Net of taxes, real effective earnings per head may have declined by 1 per cent after a rise of 2 per cent in 1983. Disposable income of households nevertheless kept growing in real terms (by 1 per cent, down from more than 3 per cent in 1983), as income from property and entrepreneurship continued to expand strongly.

Negotiations in the last pay round, which will determine developments in 1985, are taking place against the background of a markedly higher inflation rate and an improved business situation. The settlements suggest that the price push in 1984 has not left wage trends unaffected. Basic and effective wages in most groups were raised by 6 and 4¾ per cent respectively. In some sectors, where pay rises had come down less, the settlements have exceeded those of the previous round by 1½ percentage points or so. The outcome of the pay round – representing an acceleration of wage increases – may be compatible with a further improvement of profitability. In the 1983-84 round the trade unions had accepted the constraint represented by the link of the schilling to the Deutschemark. But most of the improvement will be eroded in 1985, since present wage settlements considerably exceed those in Germany and the difference is unlikely to be compensated for by higher productivity growth as happened often in the past. By contrast to Germany, the shortening of working hours will be limited in 1985 but is likely to become more general from 1986 onwards, pending the outcome of negotiations now in progress.

Balance of payments

In 1982, the current external account had improved dramatically, showing a surplus for the first time in thirteen years. Since then it has remained approximately in balance, despite a move towards deficit due mainly to a rise in the deficit on trade account (Diagram 6). In 1983, the increase in the trade deficit was attributable to a deterioration in the real foreign balance which was only partly offset by an amelioration of the terms of trade. Import volumes increased strongly in response to buoyant domestic demand, while exports, although also reviving, lagged behind. In 1984, the fall in the real foreign balance came to a halt but the favourable trend in the terms of trade since 1981 was reversed. Growth of import volumes remained relatively strong, despite a weaker expansion of domestic demand, as the demand structure shifted to components with high import content. But in the course of the year volume growth of exports caught up with that of imports, reflecting market growth as well as gains in market shares due to improving international price/cost competitiveness. The decline in relative unit labour costs and export prices in common currency accelerated from 1 per cent in 1983 to 3 per cent in 1984 (Table 4). This was mainly a consequence of a reversal of the upward trend of the effective exchange rate (Table 4). Hence, in the short run the beneficial

Diagram 6. Balance of payments developments

Billion schillings

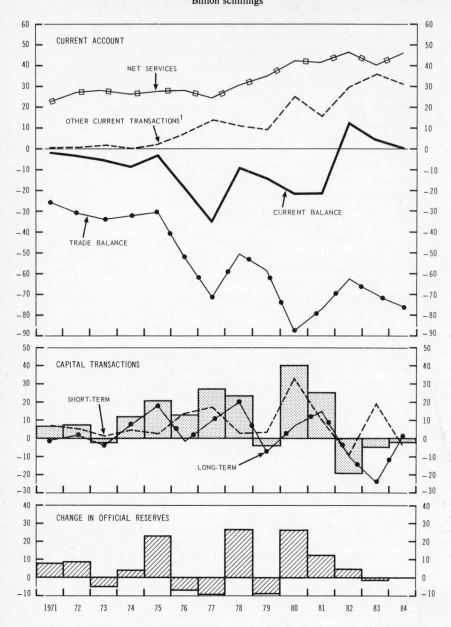

1. Deliveries not subdivisible into goods and services.
Sources: Austrian National Bank; OECD Secretariat.

Table 4. **Exchange rate development and international competitiveness**

| | Index 1970 = 100 | | | | | | | Percentage changes | | |
| | 1983 | | | | 1984 | | | | | |
	Q1	Q2	Q3	Q4	Q1	Q2	Q3	1982	1983	1984[1]
Exchange rate										
US $/Schilling	152.8	147.9	139.1	137.2	135.9	135.8	125.4	−6.8	−5.0	−9.4
DM/Schilling	100.9	100.8	100.9	100.7	100.7	100.9	101.0	0.3	−0.1	0.1
Effective exchange rate	135.5	135.0	132.9	132.4	132.6	133.6	132.7	2.0	1.4	−1.0
Relative unit labour costs										
Local currency	80.2	78.1	77.6	77.4	75.8	76.5	76.7	−3.3	−3.5	−2.3
Common currency	116.9	113.3	110.9	110.6	108.6	110.5	109.6	0.0	−1.0	−2.9
Relative consumer prices										
Local currency	77.5	76.6	76.5	76.3	77.7	77.2	..	−2.4	−2.2	..
Common currency	113.0	111.1	109.3	109.0	111.4	111.4	..	0.9	0.3	..
Relative export prices										
Local currency	66.8	66.6	65.2	65.2	64.0	64.6	64.3	−2.2	−3.5	−2.5
Common currency	97.5	96.7	93.1	93.1	91.8	93.2	91.9	1.1	−1.0	−3.0

1. Secretariat estimates.
Sources: OECD Secretariat.

impact of improved competitiveness on trade volumes was outweighed by the adverse effect of the lower exchange rate on the terms of trade.

According to customs statistics, merchandise export and import volumes rose by about 4 and 6 per cent respectively in 1983. In 1984, their growth rates, at about 10 per cent, may not have differed much. Considerably higher figures from balance of payments and national accounts statistics are strongly biased upwards, as they include transit trade which has risen dramatically in the period under review due mainly to increasing activities of a nationalised company in oil trade (in the first nine months of 1984 transit trade grew by 135 per cent compared with a year earlier, from one-fifth to two-fifths of exports as recorded by the customs statistics). While export market share gains were modest in 1983, they seem to have become more substantial in 1984. Apart from the improved price competitiveness, the relatively large share of raw materials and semi-finished goods in Austrian exports may have contributed, demand for these products being typically high at this stage of the business cycle. Strong import demand over the last year does not seem to reflect a trend rise in income elasticities of imports. The shift in the demand structure from private consumption to stockbuilding and equipment investment (with import shares of about 60 per cent) is estimated to have raised import growth by 2 percentage points. Exceptionally strong energy imports, following a decline from 1981 to 1983, also contributed. In 1983, despite an improvement of the terms of trade of 1 per cent, the deficit on trade account rose by Sch 7 billion to Sch 58½ billion (f.o.b. basis, Table 5). With this terms-of-trade gain reversed, the deterioration in the trade balance may have continued at about the same pace in 1984.

The net surplus on services and transfers, mainly stemming from tourism receipts, fell by Sch 6 billion to Sch 39 billion in 1983, as spending of Austrians abroad picked up sharply due to the marked rise in real incomes, while overnight stays of foreign visitors in Austria declined. In 1984, this trend was reversed. Although nights spent by foreigners still seem to have declined somewhat, tourism receipts recovered in value as a result of higher prices which partly reflected a shift towards higher quality. On the other hand, Austrians reduced their spending abroad as accelerating inflation adversely affected real incomes. Hence, despite a

Table 5. **Balance of payments: recent trends**

Billion schilling

	1982	1983	1983				1984		
			Q1	Q2	Q3	Q4	Q1	Q2	Q3
Seasonally adjusted[1]									
Exports (fob)	298.9	333.5	78.9	76.8	89.1	89.0	98.4	101.7	118.1
Imports (fob)	350.7	392.2	93.1	90.0	101.3	108.1	110.5	122.7	129.8
Trade balance	−51.8	−58.7	−14.2	−13.2	−12.2	−19.1	−12.1	−21.0	−11.7
Invisibles	64.0	62.7	16.2	16.9	15.3	13.9	9.8	18.5	11.1
Current balance	12.2	4.0	2.0	3.7	3.1	−5.2	−2.3	−2.4	−0.6
Not seasonally adjusted									
Current balance	12.2	4.0	7.3	−0.3	6.2	−9.2	2.1	−4.9	1.6
Total non-monetary capital[2]	−5.5	−33.7	−9.4	−12.2	−1.7	−10.3	7.6	−14.1	0.8
Balance on non-monetary transactions	6.7	−29.7	−2.0	−12.5	4.4	−19.6	9.7	−11.2	2.5
Banking short-term capital	−2.9	21.8	−0.6	8.4	−3.1	17.1	−4.3	4.8	−6.2
Balance on official settlements	3.7	−7.8	−2.7	−4.0	1.4	−2.5	5.4	−6.4	−3.8
Memorandum item:									
Total capital[2]	17.5	−8.2	7.3	−6.4	2.1	−11.2	10.2	−13.1	−0.2

1. Seasonally adjusted data are Secretariat estimates.
2. Including errors and omissions.
Sources: Oesterreichische Nationalbank, *Mitteilungen;* OECD Secretariat.

renewed rise in net interest payments due to higher interest rates and foreign debt, the surplus on net services and transfers may have moved back to about the 1982 level. With fluctuations of the surplus on "unclassified goods and services", which include goods and services associated with the trade in capital goods, largely offsetting those of net services and transfers (Diagram 6), the surplus on invisibles account seems to have remained broadly stable at Sch 60 to 65 billion since 1982 (Table 5). Reflecting all these trends, the current external account, which still achieved a slight surplus of Sch 4 billion (US $0.2 billion) in 1983, is likely to have moved into deficit in 1984. In the past, however, data revisions usually brought about an improvement so that the deficit may turn out to be smaller than now indicated by the statistics.

The capital account, which had swung into sizeable deficit in 1982 when the current account surplus and ample liquidity prompted substantial capital outflows, has been close to balance since then. Net long-term capital outflows increased further in 1983 (Diagram 6, Table 5), reflecting the continuing refinancing of export credits from domestic sources, reduced net borrowing from abroad by public authorities, and the decreasing positive long-term interest rate differential between Austria and Germany. This was, however, largely offset by sizeable net short-term capital imports by banks. In 1984, the long-term capital account swung back into surplus due mainly to increased foreign currency bond issues of banks. Public authorities raised more funds abroad but this was outweighed by net outflows on account of companies and individuals mostly through higher investment in foreign (withholding tax-exempt) bonds. As lower foreign borrowing of banks led, contrary to the year before, to net short-term capital outflows, the total capital account may have shown a slight deficit in 1984 as in 1983. Official reserves increased slightly in the year as a whole, outflows in early 1984 having been reversed after the rise in central bank interest rates in March.

III. MACROECONOMIC POLICIES AND SHORT-TERM PROSPECTS

After being expansionary in the late phase of the recession and into the first year of the recovery, the stance of economic policy has shifted towards restriction. In view of the strong rise in public debt in 1982-83, the Federal Government has taken important consolidation measures which have reversed the upward trend of the deficit/GDP ratio which had reached 5½ per cent in 1983. In the absence of further marked budget cuts, however, the increase in deficits is likely to resume in 1986. Given the exchange rate link to the Deutschemark, the easing of monetary policy had to be discontinued in mid-1983 when the downward trend of international interest rates was reversed and monetary relaxation in Germany ended. The shift in the policy stance, though, was also influenced by an acceleration in inflation, mainly due to the increase in VAT, a deterioration in the current balance and capital movements in response to tax changes (see below) leading the authorities to aim at a positive interest rate differential against Germany.

Fiscal policy

Budget consolidation had made significant progress in the early 1980s, the Federal Government deficit coming close to the medium-term objective at that time of 2½ per cent of GDP by 1981. However, given the protracted recession, the authorities in 1982 adopted two employment programmes and accepted sizeable deficit overruns. The 1983 budget plan originally aimed at a stabilisation of the deficit at the 1982 level. But in view of the continuing rise in unemployment, the Federal Government decided that part of the contingency budget should be implemented. As in 1982, though, only a relatively small portion of the overshooting of the deficit was attributable to these discretionary measures, the major part reflecting too optimistic assumptions underlying the budget.

In 1983, the Federal budget deficit (excluding debt repayments) at Sch 65.6 billion (5.4 per cent of GDP) was about Sch 17 billion (1½ per cent of GDP) higher than originally planned, with revenue and expenditure each contributing equally to the overshooting (Table 6). Instead of exceeding expenditure growth as planned, the rate of growth of total revenue (slightly over 5 per cent) remained considerably below that of expenditure (10 per cent). About one-half of the tax shortfalls can be explained by lower nominal GDP and employment than assumed, the remainder reflecting the disappointing results of a tax amnesty. Incomes from Federal enterprises were also considerably lower than expected. On the expenditure side almost two-thirds of the budget overruns reflected higher transfers to social security due to the adverse effect of higher-than-assumed unemployment on contributions and benefits. Contrary to expectations, Federal Government investment fell short of budget plans and hardly increased in real terms, as additional funds from the contingency budget were outweighed by underspending in other areas. Because of the changes in the expenditure structure towards items with a lower demand impact, the expansionary effect of the 1983 budget is likely to have been much weaker than suggested by the change in the overall budget balance. The change in the financial balance excluding those items which do not affect domestic demand (hereafter referred to as the internal-demand-effective financial balance) was about only two-thirds that of the overall balance (Table 6) and the change in the weighted budget balance, which takes account of different multiplier effects, was slightly lower again.

Concerned about the unexpectedly rapid increase in public debt and the sharp rise in the share of debt servicing in total expenditure, the Federal Government in September 1983

Table 6. The Federal Budget
Administrative basis

	1982 Outturn	1983 Voted	1983 Preliminary outturn	1984 Voted	1984 Estimated outturn	1985 Proposal	1983 outturn / 1982 outturn	1984 estimate / 1983 outturn	1985 proposal / 1984 estimate
	Billion schilling						Percentage changes		
Revenue									
1. Taxes[1]	208.8	230.0	223.3	245.1	250.3	266.4	6.9	12.1	6.4
2. Incomes from Federal enterprises	55.7	61.6	58.0	64.8	63.1	67.2	4.1	8.9	6.5
3. Other[2]	28.7	27.7	28.6	28.7	28.9	29.5	−0.3	1.0	2.1
4. Total[3] (1 to 3)	293.2	319.3	310.0	338.6	342.3	363.1	5.7	10.4	6.1
5. Total[4]	301.0	325.8	316.7	341.8	345.4	369.2	5.2	9.1	6.9
Expenditure									
6. Wages and salaries[5]	88.1	93.3	92.8	96.7	98.3	102.3	5.3	5.9	4.1
7. Gross investment	32.4	35.7	34.5	36.5	38.0	38.3	6.5	10.2	0.8
8. Investment promotion	7.0	7.9	8.2	9.4	9.4	10.7	17.1	14.6	13.8
9. Price subsidies and transfers	118.5	127.2	133.7	140.0	138.0	141.1	12.8	3.7	2.2
10. Other[6]	99.4	110.0	108.0	120.8	116.4	135.7	8.7	7.8	16.6
11. Total[7] (6 to 10)	345.4	374.2	377.2	403.4	400.1	428.1	9.2	6.1	7.0
12. Total[8]	347.6	374.2	382.3	404.0	403.4	429.7	10.0	5.5	6.5
Contingency budget	0	6.3	3.5	5.9	0	4.7			
Stabilisation quota	0	3.7	3.5	3.0	0	3.1			
Reflationary quota	0	2.6	0	2.9	0	1.6			
							Change in per cent of previous year's GDP		
Overall budget balance excluding debt repayments (5 minus 12)	−46.6	−48.4	−65.6	−62.2	−58.0	−60.5	−1.7	0.6	−0.2
Per cent of GDP	(−4.1)	(−4.0)	(−5.4)	(−4.8)	(−4.5)	(−4.4)			
Internal demand-effective financial balance[9]	−42.2	−41.0	−53.6	−48.8	−47.0	−48.6	−1.0	0.5	−0.1
Per cent of GDP	(−3.7)	(−3.4)	(−4.4)	(−3.8)	(−3.7)	(−3.5)			
Memorandum item:									
GDP at current prices (percentage changes)[10]	7.7	7.0[10]	5.9	5.5[10]	6.6	7.0[10]			

1. Including other similar levies.
2. Including interest receipts.
3. Excluding withdrawals from reserves.
4. Including withdrawals from reserves.
5. Including contribution to salaries of teachers employed by the States (Länder).
6. Including purchases and payments abroad and interest payments.
7. Excluding additions to reserves.
8. Including additions to reserves.
9. Excluding inter alia purchases and payments abroad, withdrawals and additions to reserves, and debt repayment.
10. Budget estimate.

Sources: Ministry of Finance, WIFO and Secretariat estimates.

adopted a consolidation package for the 1984 budget. Although no improvement in the economic situation was expected at that time (the budget assumption for real GDP growth and the unemployment rate in 1984 were ½ per cent and 5½ per cent, respectively), it was felt that the upward trend in the deficit had to be reversed in order to restore the room for manoeuvre of fiscal policy. This highlights the concern with which the authorities viewed the accumulated fiscal imbalances (see the final paragraph of this section), as they were prepared to take the risk of (procyclical) deflationary effects on aggregate demand. The consolidation measures comprised mainly tax increases which were estimated to raise revenue in 1984 by about 1 per cent of GDP. In particular, VAT rates were increased by 2 percentage points as from January 1984, along with other taxes, fiscal charges and social security contributions. A new tax on interest accruing from schilling deposits and newly issued bonds was introduced which, however, will not greatly affect the Budget before 1985. On the other hand, the burden for business of taxes not related to profits was reduced. Tax receipts and total revenues were thus expected to rise by 10 and 8 per cent respectively. Cuts on the expenditure side, including a small reduction in social benefits, were moderate, but expenditure growth was intended to be limited to projected nominal GDP growth (5½ per cent). The Federal budget deficit was projected to drop to Sch 62 billion (less than 5 per cent of GDP) in 1984.

Unlike the year before, economic developments in 1984 were more favourable than assumed in the Budget (nominal GDP growth would seem to have been more than 1 percentage point higher and the unemployment rate 1 percentage point lower) and therefore a larger fall in the deficit could be expected. Recent estimates suggest that the Federal Government deficit in 1984 at 4½ per cent of GDP was significantly lower than voted in December 1983 (Table 6). In particular, tax receipts would seem to have been markedly higher than projected. Overall expenditure is estimated to have been much as planned. Social transfers expanded less than expected, due to the more favourable labour market situation than assumed in the Budget. The resulting budget savings were, however, reduced by additions to the unemployment reserve fund. On the other hand, as in the previous year, there were additional payments for agriculture support and export promotion. Investment, which fell short of budget plans in the year before, seems to have exceeded projections in 1984 due to the catch-up in delays in the implementation of some projects, apparently also growing in volume for the first time since the late 1970s. And government expenditure on wages and salaries was considerably higher than planned. Given these changes in the structure of expenditures and the fact that the reduction of the deficit owed much to revenue increases which have a lower direct demand impact than expenditure cuts, the restrictive impact of Federal Government finances in 1984, as measured by the change in the weighted budget balance, seems to have been much smaller than indicated by the change in the overall and internal demand-effective balance (Table 6).

The Federal Budget for 1985 is designed to pursue the consolidation efforts of the previous year but without further tax increases. Expenditure growth is to be kept below the projected growth rate of nominal GDP (7 per cent). This deceleration of expenditure growth (Table 6) is mainly the result of the first step of a pension insurance reform which aims at containing the Federal transfer to the pension funds through higher contributions of employees and employers. Investment, too, is projected to rise only slightly compared with the estimated outcome for 1984. Investment incentives, however, are budgeted to be raised substantially. Revenue is projected to rise slightly less than nominal GDP. The tax burden of business will fall further due to measures introduced the year before. On the other hand, the new tax on interest incomes will provide sizeable additional receipts in 1985 (the reduction of the tax rate from 7½ to 5 per cent will mainly affect the 1986 Budget). On the basis of official projections, which are for a slight drop in the Federal budget deficit as well as the internal

Table 7. **Fiscal policy indicators**
National accounts basis

	1979	1980	1981	1982	1983	1984	1985
	Percentage changes						
Expenditure							
Central government	7.8	6.0	8.8	11.0	9.6	7.8	6.0
General government	7.2	8.2	9.3	8.1	6.3	6.4	6.6
Revenue							
Central government	10.3	8.0	10.4	3.6	6.2	11.3	7.2
General government	8.0	9.8	9.7	4.9	5.7	8.2	7.6
	Per cent of GDP						
Expenditure							
General government	48.2	48.1	49.5	49.8	50.0	49.8	49.6
Revenue							
General government	45.8	46.4	48.0	46.7	46.6	47.2	47.4
Net lending							
Central government	−3.0	−2.6	−2.3	−4.0	−4.9	−4.2	−3.9
General government	−2.4	−1.7	−1.6	−3.1	−3.4	−2.6	−2.2
Cyclically adjusted	−1.7	−1.2	−0.0	−0.7	−1.3	−0.9	−1.2
Changes in net lending							
General government	+0.4	+0.7	+0.1	−1.5	−0.3	+0.8	+0.4
Discretionary	−0.8	+0.5	+1.2	−0.7	−0.6	+0.4	−0.3
Built-in stabilisers	+1.2	+0.2	−1.1	−0.8	+0.3	+0.4	+0.7
	Percentage changes						
Memorandum items:							
Nominal GDP	9.0	8.3	6.2	7.7	5.9	6.6	6.9
Real GDP	4.7	3.0	−0.1	1.0	2.1	2.2	3.0
Real potential output	2.4	2.5	1.9	2.5	1.4	1.5	2.0
Capacity utilisation	2.2	0.5	−2.0	−1.5	0.7	0.8	1.0

Sources: Ministry of Finance, WIFO and Secretariat estimates.

demand-effective financial balance in relation to GDP, the impact of the Federal budget on the growth of aggregate demand in 1985 would seem to be broadly neutral. With revenue estimates rather cautious, a more pronounced fall in the deficit cannot be excluded, depending, however, on a containment of expenditure overruns. Recent wage settlements suggest that expenditure on wages and salaries may be higher than planned. And investment outlays may again exceed projections as there still appear to be delays in the implementation of programmes from the 1982/83 period.

As the Federal authorities' scope for influencing the fiscal behaviour of local governments is limited (a change in the Constitution which would increase co-ordination between different levels of government is being discussed in Parliament), the impact of total public sector transactions on economic activity may deviate considerably from that of the Federal Budget. In 1982-83, when Federal government spending rose sharply due to the compensatory fiscal policy (Table 7), non-central government (including social security) expenditure, which accounts for about one-half of total public spending (50 per cent of GDP), expanded less than both nominal GDP and local government revenue. In 1984, in spite of the shift of Federal government policy towards restriction, local government expenditure growth seems to have remained below average, and this trend will be reversed only in 1985, according to budget projections. The burden of expenditure restraint has fallen heavily on public investment, the bulk of which is undertaken by local authorities. Thus, notwithstanding buoyant Federal government investment, total public investment seems to have continued to decline in volume, though at a slower pace. With the traditional financial surplus of non-central government[1] rising markedly from 1981 to 1983, the increase in the public sector deficit in this period by about 2 percentage points to 3½ per cent of GDP remained significantly below that of central government (Table 7). In 1984 the general government net borrowing requirement is estimated to have dropped to about 2½ per cent of GDP and, on the basis of budget projections, a further slight fall seems likely in 1985. According to OECD

Diagram 7. **Covernment debt**

GENERAL GOVERNMENT LIABILITIES
In per cent of GDP

OECD

AUSTRIA

FEDERAL GOVERNMENT DEBT SERVICING
In per cent of net tax revenues

TOTAL

INTEREST PAYMENTS

1974 75 76 77 78 79 80 81 82 83 84 85

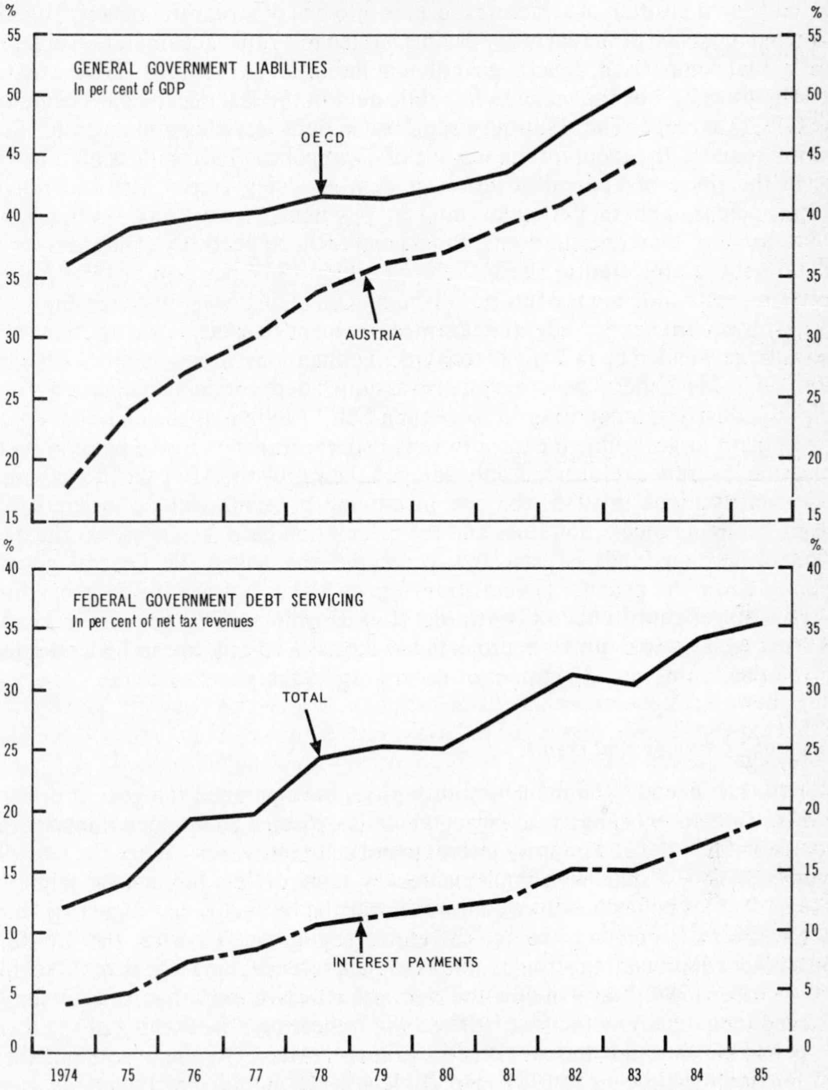

Sources: Österreichische Postsparkasse; OECD Secretariat.

27

estimates, and disregarding the effects of built-in stabilisers, the negative swing in the public sector deficit in the two years 1982 and 1983 together exceeded 1 per cent of GDP, implying a discretionary easing of fiscal policy. Of the projected fall in the deficit in 1984 about one-half – i.e. 0.4 per cent of GDP – is estimated to be the result of restrictive policy measures, the remainder being due to cyclical developments (Table 7). In 1985, the positive impact of the economic recovery on public sector finances would seem to exceed the projected fall in the deficit, implying an expansionary stance of fiscal policy. But as the time lags involved may be underestimated and there is a possibility that the fall in the deficit may be stronger than projected, any results of such calculations should be interpreted cautiously.

As a consequence of stimulative fiscal measures in the mid-1970s public sector finances have moved from a position of structural surplus into one of structural deficit. Together with the protracted recession of the early 1980s, this has led to a rapid accumulation of public debt. By international comparison, general government liabilities in relation to GDP are still below average (Diagram 7), but the increase in public debt in the last decade has been more rapid than the OECD average. The resulting strong rise in debt servicing and its costs has already significantly reduced the room for manoeuvre of fiscal policy. This is illustrated by the sharp increase in the share of Federal government debt servicing (repayment of principal plus interest payments), and in particular interest payments, in net tax revenues since the mid-1970s, to more than one-third and almost one-fifth, respectively (Diagram 7). In 1985, the Federal debt is projected to rise to Sch 531 billion (38½ per cent of GDP), implying a substantial interest burden in the future. Off-budget financing has also increasingly burdened budgets in subsequent years. Federal guarantees on loans to special construction companies, which have largely ended up in *de facto* repayment obligations, amounted to Sch 40 billion by the end of 1983. The Federal government also assumed debt servicing obligations for loans to nationalised industries, amounting to more than Sch 17 billion at the end of 1983. Another dynamic element in government expenditure is Federal transfers to the pension funds[2]. The recent pension insurance reform has only damped their growth. After the increase in pension insurance contributions in 1985, the rise in old-age pensions will be lowered from 1986 onwards by changing indexation rules and the calculation base. Nevertheless the increase in the deficit of pension funds is projected to resume and, given the Federal government's obligation to cover the deficits, Federal transfers as a share of the funds' expenditure may again exceed 30 per cent from 1987 onwards, after dropping to 27½ per cent in 1985. On the basis of these trends, medium-term projections suggest a steady rise in Federal government deficits, even assuming no adjustment of fiscal drag in the years to come.

Monetary policy, money and credit

Over the last decade, the monetary authorities have pursued the goal of price stability mainly by setting an exchange rate target which is expected to dampen imported inflation, limit pay rises and in the end improve international competitiveness. Since the late 1970s this "hard-currency policy" has been implemented by more or less linking the schilling to the Deutschemark. This policy has been continued over the last year, exchange rate movements against the German currency being, therefore, negligible. Vis-à-vis the US dollar, the schilling has kept depreciating strongly, the exchange rate reaching a peak of 22 schillings per dollar in October 1984. Nevertheless the nominal effective exchange rate of the schilling strengthened temporarily in the first half of 1984, reflecting a weakening of the Swiss franc and the pound sterling, but has weakened again thereafter. On the average of the year, it dropped for the first time since 1981 (see Table 4 in the Balance of Payments section).

The "hard-currency option" implies that short-term interest rates are kept broadly in line with German interest rates to avoid pressures on the schilling/Deutschemark exchange rate through capital movements. In parallel with international rates, Austria's interest rates fell until the second quarter of 1983, the decline having been accompanied by a strong expansion of the central bank money stock and bank liquidity. When international rates began to drift upwards, monetary policy had to be tightened again. The shift in the policy stance was also influenced by domestic developments. Expectations of the tax changes (introduction of a new tax on interest revenues[3] and rise in VAT rates) prompted capital outflows and also a deterioration of the current account position due to advanced consumer spending. Contrary to expectations, these trends were not reversed in early 1984, as import demand remained relatively buoyant and capital outflows continued: after the introduction of the witholding tax the hike in interest rates was apparently considered insufficient. The resulting loss of currency reserves together with the growing inflation differential against Germany induced the Central Bank to raise the discount rate by ½ percentage point to 4¼ per cent and the Lombard rate by ¾ percentage point to 5½ per cent in March 1984. In late June the discount rate was raised by a further ¼ percentage point to 4½ per cent concurrent with a similar move of the German monetary authorities. With these adjustments Central Bank rates were back at German levels, after having been below those in 1983 when the improved external balance position had increased the room for manoeuvre of monetary policy.

The marked tightening of monetary policy since mid-1983 has brought about a considerable rise in short-term interest rates. In December 1984, the call money rate at 7½ per cent was 3 percentage points above the level of May 1983, when the fall in interest rates came to an end (Diagram 8). The positive differential against German rates, which was negligible in 1981-83, began widening at the turn of 1984 to reach more than 1 percentage point in the second half of 1984. Long-term interest rates, which are less influenced by monetary policy, have fluctuated little. In December 1984 the bond yield in the secondary market at about 8 per cent was practically unchanged from mid-1983, about 1 percentage point higher than in Germany. This differential began to emerge only in 1984 due to a fall in German rates; Austrian interest rates may be expected to respond with a lag to German developments. The new tax on interest revenues affects only bonds issued since January 1984. Since the second quarter, the yield of new issues has therefore been ½ percentage point above the bond yield in the secondary market, the difference corresponding to the tax burden. Given the ongoing public discussion and pressure by the banking community, the Government decided in October 1984 to lower the rate to 5 per cent from January 1985 onwards. Real interest rate – as measured by the difference between the bond yield on the secondary market and the year-on-year rise in the consumer price index – was drifting downwards since summer 1983 from its high level of more than 5½ per cent to about 4 per cent at the end of that year. The strong rise in consumer prices in early 1984 due to the VAT-rate increase pushed down real rates by a further 2 percentage points to a level of somewhat above 2 per cent. Given the temporary nature of the price acceleration, however, this measure is likely to overstate the decline in real interest rates.

With interest rates being intermediate targets to support the exchange rate goal, money supply is largely endogenous, changing according to interest rate needs, and, therefore, mirrors developments abroad, notably in Germany. After accelerating for two years, growth of the Central Bank money stock peaked in the first half of 1983 (Table 8 and Diagram 9). Since then it slowed sharply to 2½ per cent in 1984. Capital outflows led to a decline in net foreign assets of the National Bank. Up to mid-1983 their fall had been outweighed by a rise in net domestic assets, mainly through additional rediscount and Lombard credit. Open market operations contributed only little. Strong expansion of monetary aggregates in 1983 partly reversed the rise in velocity of circulation during the high interest period of the early 1980s.

Diagram 8. Interest rates

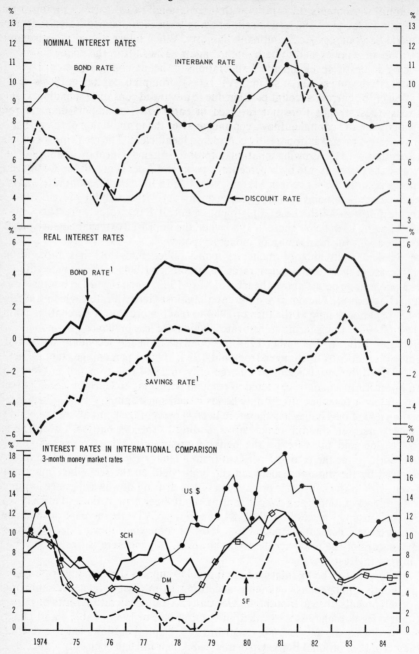

1. Nominal rate minus change in consumer price index (quarterly, year-on-year).
Source: OECD Secretariat.

Diagram 9. Monetary indicators[1]

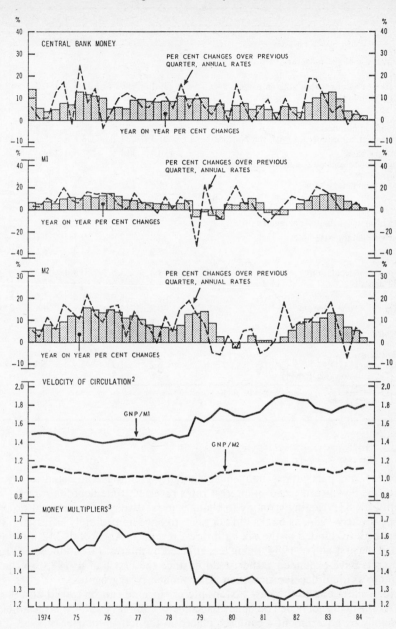

1. Monetary aggregates in the definition of the Österreichisches Institut für Wirtschaftsforschung.
2. Quarterly GNP over M1 and M2, respectively.
3. M1 over adjusted monetary base.
Sources: Österreichisches Institut für Wirtschaftsforschung; OECD Secretariat.

Table 8. Monetary developments

	1981	1982	1983	1983 I	1983 II	1984 I
	Schilling billion					
A. Source and use of the monetary base						
Sources						
Net foreign assets of the Nationalbank	89.1	98.5	99.5	100.3	98.6	92.6
Net domestic assets	21.3	20.3	28.1	23.7	32.6	36.4
Use						
Currency in circulation	79.2	81.6	89.5	86.9	92.0	89.2
Commercial banks deposits with the Nationalbank	31.3	37.2	38.1	37.1	39.2	39.7
Monetary base	110.4	118.8	127.6	124.0	131.2	129.0
Adjustment for changes in minimum reserve requirements	−4.1	−4.8	−7.6	−7.7	−7.5	−7.6
Adjusted monetary base	114.6	123.6	135.2	131.7	138.7	136.6
	Per cent, seasonally adjusted annual rates					
B. Growth of main monetary aggregates[1]						
Adjusted monetary base	5.3	7.9	9.3	16.6	4.4	2.8
M1	2.2	2.3	13.4	16.6	10.8	1.9
Of which:						
Currency in circulation[2]	3.4	3.0	10.3	14.3	7.6	−1.8
Sight deposits	1.2	1.6	16.3	18.8	13.7	5.2
M2	1.0	6.7	11.6	10.9	14.0	−1.3
Of which: Time deposits	−0.9	14.3	8.9	1.1	24.0	−9.6
M3	9.7	13.8	11.2	11.5	9.6	4.3
Of which: Saving deposits	14.8	17.3	10.9	11.3	7.5	7.0
Memorandum items:						
Growth of nominal GDP	6.2	7.7	5.9	5.2	8.5	5.8
Velocity of circulation (GDP/M1)	3.8	5.3	−6.6	−9.9	−2.2	4.1

1. M1, M2 and M3 as defined by the Oesterreichisches Institut für Wirtschaftsforschung which exclude deposits with the Nationalbank.
2. Excluding gold and silver coins.
Sources: WIFO; OECD Secretariat.

Growth of M1 was particularly buoyant as liquidity preference adjusted to lower interest rates. With the downward trend in interest rates reversed, time deposits rose rapidly in the second half of 1983, reacting strongly to changes in relative asset prices, but dropped again temporarily in early 1984, as banks did not seem to have immediately adjusted time deposit rates after the introduction of the tax on interest revenues. As a result M2 was particularly depressed in the first half of 1984. Being less affected by interest rate-induced portfolio shifts, saving deposits have expanded rather steadily since the first half of 1983, so that M3 has shown a more gradual deceleration than other monetary aggregates.

Portfolio shifts due to the new tax on interest income can be traced also in the credit markets. As the tax is not levied on bonds issued before January 1984, a large amount of new issues – mainly by government – could be placed in the fourth quarter of 1983. Part of the accruing liquidity has been held by the Federal Government on time deposit accounts for later use. As a result of advanced placements and weak demand after the introduction of the withholding tax there were no bond issues until March 1984, and from January to October 1984 their amount was only half that of the year before. The Government has continued to take up a large part of funds needed in the form of bank credit. Besides consumer

Table 9. **Financial balances**

Per cent of GDP

	1974	1975	1976	1977	1980	1981	1982	1983	1984[1]
Private households	4.8	6.2	6.6	5.0	6.1	4.8	5.3	4.4	5.5
Public sector	1.3	−2.5	−3.7	−2.4	−1.7	−1.6	−3.1	−3.4	−2.6
Non-bank enterprises	−7.0	−3.8	−5.1	−6.3	−7.1	−5.3	−1.2	−0.9	−3.0
External sector	1.0	0.1	2.3	3.6	2.7	2.0	−1.1	−0.1	0.1

1. Estimate.
Sources: Austrian Central Statistical Office; OECD Secretariat.

credit this was a major source of bank credit expansion. Credit demand of the other sectors remained weak until spring 1984 and has picked up somewhat subsequently. Weak credit demand of the enterprise sector since 1982 is due to a pronounced, albeit uneven, recovery of profits, which has improved cash-flow, combined with depressed investment activity. As a result, the net debtor position of enterprises as a per cent of GDP reached a historical low in 1983. Since late 1984, however, strengthening investment demand raised the need for external funds. Nevertheless, the net debtor position of the enterprise sector is likely to remain low compared to the upswing following the first oil crisis (Table 9). The deterioration of government financial balances as a per cent of GDP was far less pronounced during the last recession than in the mid-1970s. Reflecting the weaker economic expansion, however, the subsequent consolidation efforts also did not ameliorate the Government's financial position to the same extent. The major change compared to the 1970s concerns the external position which was balanced in 1983 and 1984, while it moved into considerable deficit between 1975 and 1977, the difference being due mainly to a weaker growth in the current upswing but also to a more favourable development of the competitive position than in the mid-1970s.

Short-term prospects

The economic recovery in the OECD area is projected to continue over the next eighteen months at a slower pace, with growth differentials narrowing. Real GDP is forecast to expand at an annual rate of about 3 per cent, reflecting a moderation of growth in the United States and broadly unchanged modest growth in Europe (at a rate of around 2½ per cent). Growth of world trade volumes may gradually slow down to an annual rate of around 5 per cent. Given the adjustment that has taken place in non-OECD countries, their import demand may begin to grow again. Nevertheless, intra-OECD trade again seems likely to expand faster than world trade. However, reflecting the importance of European countries with below average growth for Austria's foreign trade, its export market growth may be somewhat slower than world trade developments, coming down from an annual rate of more than 7 per cent in the second half of 1984 to one of about 4½ per cent in the first half of 1986. With the real exchange rate dropping by about 3 per cent in 1984 and likely to decline further in the period ahead under the usual assumption of constant nominal exchange rates, substantial market gains can be expected due to the improved competitive position. Hence, volume growth of merchandise exports is projected to exceed that of markets by 3 to 4 percentage points. Due mainly to the continuing weakness of tourism receipts, total exports seem likely to expand at a slower pace. Even so the volume of exports of goods and services may increase by more than 8 per cent through 1985 and reach about 6 per cent (s.a.a.r.) in the first half of 1986.

The policy environment has been described in some detail above. Given the exchange rate

Diagram 10. Leading indicators

Seasonally adjusted quarterly data

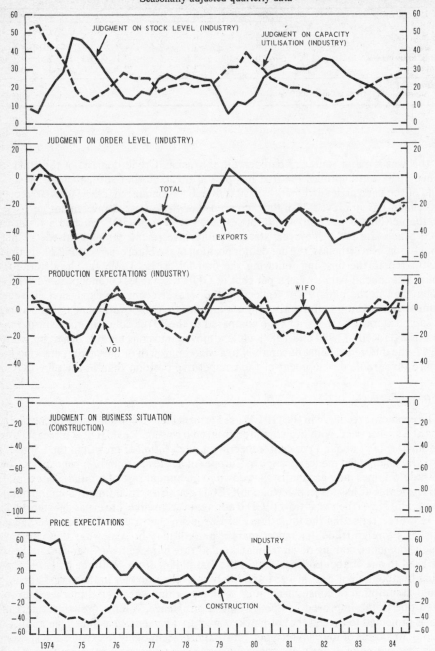

Sources: WIFO; Vereinigung Österreichischer Industrieller (VÖI); OECD Secretariat.

link, monetary policy is assumed to keep interest rates slightly above those in Germany which are expected to remain fairly stable up to 1986. After adopting the important consolidation measures in 1984, the Federal Government intends to pursue the same policy approach in 1985 but without further tax increases and by keeping expenditure growth below the projected growth rate of nominal GDP. This policy stance is assumed to be continued in 1986. The general government net borrowing requirement is projected to fall from about 2½ per cent of GDP in 1984 to about 2 per cent in 1986. This would seem to imply a neutral or slightly expansionary policy stance as the working of built-in stabilisers is estimated to entail a move towards surplus (see fiscal policy section above).

Leading indicators available at the end of 1984 suggest that the recovery has gathered momentum again after the policy-induced slowdown in the first half of 1984. As evidenced by the survey data summarised in Diagram 11, the business situation has improved, particularly in industry, which has been less affected by the budget consolidation measures because of buoyant foreign demand. With export demand continuing strong and domestic demand recovering, real GDP growth is expected to accelerate from somewhat more than 2 per cent in 1984 to about 3 per cent in 1985 (Table 10). The rebound of domestic demand mainly reflects a revival of private consumption, which had been most affected by fiscal measures. The expansion of fixed capital formation, too, is projected to accelerate, albeit much less, while restocking, the mainstay of domestic demand growth in 1984, is not expected to contribute significantly further to GDP growth. As a result, import growth is forecast to decelerate and the positive GDP contribution of the real foreign balance to rise somewhat (growth rates of both imports and exports in 1984 shown in Table 10 are strongly biased

Table 10. **Short-term prospects**

	1982		Percentage changes in volume terms (1976 prices)			
	Current prices Bill. Sch.	% of GDP	1983	1984	1985	1986 I / 1985 I
Private consumption	642.9	56.5	5.0	−1	2	2¼
Government consumption	214.3	18.8	2.0	2	2	2
Gross fixed capital formation	262.8	23.1	−1.9	3	4	3½
Of which:						
Construction	152.7	13.4	−0.8	−1¼	3	2
Machinery and equipment	110.2	9.7	−3.2	8¼	5¼	5¼
Final domestic demand	1 120.0	98.4	2.8	½	2½	2½
Stockbuilding[1, 2]	−0.7	−0.1	0.6	1¼	0	−0
Total domestic demand	1 119.3	97.7	3.5	2	2½	2½
Exports of goods and services	463.3	40.7	6.2	14½	6¾	7
Imports of goods and services	444.5	39.1	9.9	14½	5½	6½
Foreign balance[1]	18.8	1.7	−1.2	¼	¾	½
GDP at constant prices			2.1	2¼	3	2¾
GDP price deflator			3.7	4½	3¾	4
GDP at current prices	1 138.1	100.0	5.9	6½	7	7
Memorandum items:						
Consumer prices[3]			3.2	5¾	4	4
Industrial production			0.9	4½	3½	3
Unemployment[4]			4.1	4¼	4	4
Current balance (US$ billion)			0.2	−0	0	0

1. Rates of change as a percentage of GDP in the previous period.
2. Including statistical difference.
3. Implicit consumption deflator.
4. In per cent of total labour force.
Source: OECD Secretariat.

upwards due to an enormous rise in transit trade, see Balance of Payments section above). Real GDP growth may drop a little in 1986 with a slowdown in the increase of net exports.

With the effects of VAT-related pre-buying petering out and real income growth accelerating, real private consumption is forecast to grow by 2 per cent in 1985 after a fall of 1 per cent in 1984. Despite accelerating wage increases and the pick-up in employment, the expansion of disposable income of households is projected to slow in nominal terms as a result of fiscal drag and higher social security contributions. The decline in the inflation rate after the VAT-induced price push in 1984 should, however, lead to some acceleration of disposable income growth in real terms. Following the strong fluctuations mainly related to the VAT increase, the saving ratio should decline somewhat in 1985 after the sharp rise in the year before. The drop in the ratio could be even more pronounced than assumed in the projections, given the large amount of bonus-carrying saving deposits to be deblocked in 1985. In the absence of important fiscal measures, growth of real consumer demand can be expected to accelerate slightly into 1986. The projected rise in the growth rate of real gross fixed capital formation (Table 10) is the result of diverging short- and medium-term trends for investment in equipment and structures. The expansion of machinery and equipment investment is expected to decelerate after the strong advance in the first half of 1984 but to remain above average. Improving profitability and capacity utilisation should in particular lead to a rebound of industrial investment which so far has lagged behind. Construction investment, on the other hand, would seem to have recovered somewhat after the drop in the first half of 1984, reflecting in part the VAT rise, to show a volume increase in 1985 for the first time in six years. The medium-term outlook for construction, however, is less favourable. Survey data show only a hesitant improvement of the business situation (Diagram 10), and public investment, which seems to have supported construction activity in the recent past, must be expected to turn down again, in view of continuing budget consolidation efforts.

The projected expansion of output should lead to a continuing slight rise in employment. The unemployment rate is not, however, expected to drop significantly from its present level, as growth of the labour force is also likely to accelerate, reflecting the slower net emigration of foreigners and a diminishing discouraged worker effect in the course of the recovery. Inflation is projected to come down to about 4 per cent. The rise in the inflation rate in 1984 contributed to higher wage settlements for 1985. Nevertheless, unit labour cost increases are expected to remain moderate. Under the assumption of constant exchange rates, import prices should rise markedly less than in 1984. Although the increase in export prices is expected to be somewhat lower than that of import prices, the current external account is projected to remain broadly in a position of equilibrium, as the improvement in the real foreign balance is expected to roughly match the deterioration of the terms of trade.

IV. SOME ASPECTS OF STRUCTURAL ADJUSTMENT IN INDUSTRY

Although Austria's overall economic performance has continued to compare favourably with many Member countries, structural problems have emerged in the period of slower growth since the mid-1970s. The authorities' concern about this development is evidenced by their commissioning of a Report on Structural Change. Given Austria's high and rising dependence on foreign trade, it is of particular interest to assess the extent to which fundamental structural adjustment has taken place in the industrial sector of the economy. For historical reasons industrial production was concentrated in labour-intensive consumer goods industries and basic goods industries after World War II. In the 1950s and 1960s, capacity grew rapidly in these sectors, as enterprises profited from strong international demand, low labour costs and a favourable exchange rate. With wage inflation accelerating and competition by less developed countries intensifying, structural problems emerged, but adjustment was facilitated by rapid economic expansion, particularly in the late 1960s and early 1970s. The strong rise in raw material and energy prices and slower economic expansion in the last decade again reinforced the importance of faster structural adjustment. This part of the Survey examines the main features of structural change in industry in international comparison, tries to identify existing structural weaknesses and special factors hampering structural change, and concludes with a review of industrial policies, in particular of government intervention in the form of subsidies and tax concessions.

Value added of the manufacturing sector as a per cent of GDP (almost 30 per cent in 1983) is high by international standards (Table 11). In the 1960s, the ratio was exceeded only by Germany's and, despite the marked drop in recent years, in 1982 there were still only four OECD countries (Japan, Germany, Italy and Portugal) which had a higher share of manufacturing value added in GDP than Austria. Hence, in spite of the importance of the tourism trade, the share of the service sector is still below the OECD average, although the difference has diminished significantly since the 1960s. The decline of the manufacturing sector's share in nominal output largely reflected movements of relative prices. In real terms, it rose until the early 1970s and fell somewhat afterwards. In the last two decades real output of the manufacturing sector has grown on average broadly in line with that of the OECD area. After a period of slower expansion than in other OECD countries in the 1960s a positive growth differential emerged at the turn of the 1970s. This prevailed in the last decade when output growth decelerated generally elsewhere.

Table 11. **Manufacturing sector's performance in international comparison**

	1960-67	1968-73	1974-79	1980-82	1960-82
	Per cent				
Share of nominal value added in GDP					
Austria	34.5	32.8	28.7	27.3	31.6
OECD Europe	30.9	29.7	28.5	26.1	29.3
Total OECD	29.4	28.1	26.6	24.7	27.7
Share of employment in total employment					
Austria	32.5	32.5	31.2	30.1	31.8
OECD Europe	27.9	28.3	27.1	25.2	27.4
Total OECD	26.9	27.2	25.4	23.7	26.1
	1960-68	1968-73	1973-79	1979-82	1960-82
	Average percentage rates of change				
Growth of real value added					
Austria	4.5	7.4	2.7	0.6	4.1
OECD Europe	5.8	6.1	1.9	−0.9	3.9
Total OECD	6.3	6.0	2.4	0.0	4.3
Growth of real value added per person employed					
Austria	5.2	6.0	3.6	2.5	4.8
OECD Europe	5.3	5.3	2.8	1.9	4.1
Total OECD	4.7	5.1	2.8	2.2	3.9

Source: *OECD Economic Outlook: Historical Statistics, 1960-1982*, Paris, 1984.

By contrast to output growth, productivity growth in the manufacturing sector has been above the OECD average in all sub-periods shown in Table 11. The favourable performance can be attributed to some extent to stronger output expansion since the late 1960s, which allowed Austrian industry to benefit from scale effects, but also to catch-up effects given the relatively low initial productivity levels in the early 1960s. Unlike developments in the OECD, industrial employment declined in the early 1960s. It was only during the strong 1968-73 recovery period that the number of employed in the manufacturing sector grew. In the last decade it has dropped again, the decrease being about the same as the OECD average. Some slowdown in the decline of agricultural employment as well as the high capacity of the service sector (especially tourism, banking and government) to absorb labour, prevented a fall in total employment in the period of slower growth since the mid-1970s (see Annex Table 1). In spite of weaker long-term employment trends in industry than abroad, the share of industrial employment in total is still considerably higher than in the OECD area as a whole (Table 11).

In response to the changes in the economic environment, the structure of manufacturing output has changed considerably in the last two decades. As noted above and evidenced by less favourable output and employment trends than abroad (Table 11), Austria's industry faced its first post-war adjustment difficulties in the 1960s when its comparative cost advantage was eroded and awareness of structural problems emerged[4]. Since the mid-1970s the problems it is confronted with have been the same as in other advanced industrial countries: high labour costs compared with newly industrialised countries, the rise in raw materials and energy prices, and slower economic expansion which in itself increased competitive pressures. The abovementioned factors have favoured the production of technology and research-intensive goods: the share of fabricated metals, machinery and equipment in manufacturing output rose from about one-fourth in 1964 to more than one-third in 1982 (Table 12). Chemical industries' output, ranging from basic to very sophisticated goods, expanded broadly in line with the total, a marked rise in their share in real terms up to 1973 having been mostly reversed later on. The production of basic products (wood, paper, non-metallic minerals and basic metals) lost ground. The same is true for traditional consumer goods industries, where the share of textiles and clothing industries fell considerably, while that of food industries hardly changed. Changes in the economic environment have not only caused pronounced changes in the output structure, but certainly also led to the adoption of more advanced production techniques in basic and traditional consumer goods industries.

Evidence points to a slower pace of structural change in industry in the period after the first oil shock. This was to some extent unavoidable given the decline in overall economic

Table 12. **The composition of manufacturing output**

Per cent

		1964	1973	1982	1964	1973	1982
		Current prices			Constant prices		
1.	Food, beverages and tobacco	16.9	15.9	16.0	15.7	16.0	16.4
2.	Textiles, wearing apparel, leather	14.2	10.9	8.0	12.6	10.5	8.4
3.	Wood and wood products	7.5	7.9	7.2	8.3	6.8	6.9
4.	Paper and paper products	7.6	6.5	6.6	8.0	6.9	6.7
5.	Chemicals	13.5	13.7	13.5	12.3	14.2	12.9
6.	Non-metallic mineral products	7.5	6.4	5.8	6.2	5.9	5.7
7.	Basic metal industries	8.0	8.4	7.7	9.5	7.9	7.1
8.	Fabricated metal products, machinery and equipment	24.8	30.3	35.1	27.1	31.8	35.9

Source: Austrian Central Statistical Office.

growth. (Lower income growth, for example, slows the speed of diversification of consumer demand.) But it also appears that the Austrian econonomy has not sufficiently adjusted to the new environment created by the two oil shocks. Measures of the speed of structural change have to be interpreted with caution, as aggregation conceals intra-industry and intra-firm developments. Nevertheless, according to a study of the WIFO Institute[5], which applies several indicators[6] to various aggregates (including employment and foreign trade) structural change slowed in the 1970s compared with the 1960s, the only exception being investment (see also below). When these same indicators are applied to more disaggregated data, the picture is modified but not reversed. Some evidence for the slowdown of structural change at the firm level is also provided by statistics on foundations and closures of enterprises (Annex Table 2). In the period of strong growth in the early 1970s, not only the number of foundations but also that of closures of establishments was high. But in the upswing following the first oil crisis the number of closures was sharply lower than in the previous recovery.

Measures of the speed of structural adjustment do not, however, indicate whether it has gone in the "right" direction. Sectoral data indicate that the structure of manufacturing has shifted away from labour- and energy-intensive branches to technology-intensive industries. This is presumably a shift in a desirable direction, but a question remains as to whether the change was sufficient. Some indications of whether structural change was sufficient may be given by comparing the Austrian experience with foreign developments. On the hypothesis that every country passes through similar stages of structural developments, a comparison with more advanced countries can show whether Austria has been able to improve its output structure relative to these economies and to what extent structural deficiencies still persist. Diagram 11 shows differences of sectoral shares in value added of manufacturing between Austria on the one hand and Germany and Sweden on the other. Vis-à-vis Germany, the largest negative difference is still that for fabricated metal products, machinery and equipment. The negative difference for chemicals even widened. Basic metal industries had a larger share in Germany in the early 1960s, but the latter shrank faster there than in Austria. The positive difference for non-metallic mineral products between Austria and Germany changed only little over the last twenty years. The same is true for wood and paper industries. For textiles, clothing and food industries, positive differences prevailed over the last twenty years, with the difference in the food industries rising and that of textiles and clothing industries diminishing somewhat. The comparison with Sweden reveals a picture similar to that just described, with a few exceptions. Wood and paper industries are favoured by natural endowments in Austria as well as in Sweden. The difference in the wood industries' share has been small. The paper industry's share has been higher in Sweden, the difference even growing over the last twenty years. The share of chemical industries has been even smaller in Sweden than in Austria, but has risen faster, so that the difference nearly halved. The sum of absolute differences – the change of which may be seen as a crude measure of the relative speed of structural change – remained broadly unchanged between 1964 and 1982, meaning that on average Austria did not catch up with either Germany or Sweden. Summarising, it can be said that the substantial structural change that had taken place in Austria in the last two decades generally went in the same direction as in the reference countries but was not significantly faster. Hence, the Austrian industrial structure, characterised by a relatively large share of labour-intensive consumer goods and basic goods industries, may still be seen as having much scope for adjustment.

As shown above (Table 11) the Austrian manufacturing sector did well in terms of productivity growth by international comparison. In a recent study the WIFO Institute[7] compared the development of the eight ISIC sub-divisions of the manufacturing sector in twelve countries from 1964 to 1981 (and in two sub-periods: 1964-1973 and 1973-81).

Diagram 11. **The output structure in international comparison**

Differences of Austrian sectoral shares in manufacturing output against Germany and Sweden

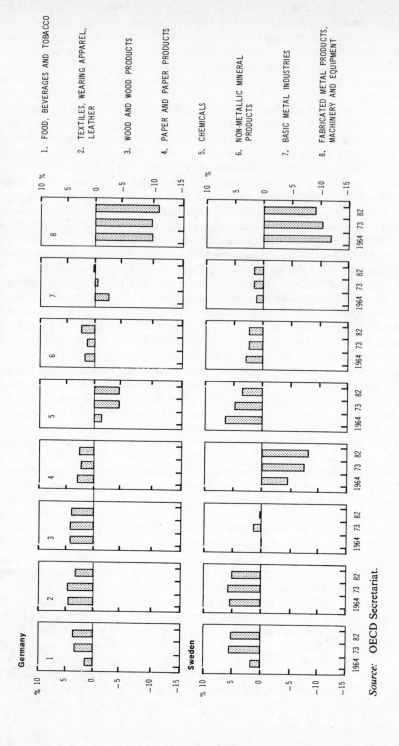

1. FOOD, BEVERAGES AND TOBACCO

2. TEXTILES, WEARING APPAREL, LEATHER

3. WOOD AND WOOD PRODUCTS

4. PAPER AND PAPER PRODUCTS

5. CHEMICALS

6. NON-METALLIC MINERAL PRODUCTS

7. BASIC METAL INDUSTRIES

8. FABRICATED METAL PRODUCTS, MACHINERY AND EQUIPMENT

Source: OECD Secretariat.

40

Compared with these countries Austria experienced a sharp deceleration of productivity growth in the basic metals and chemical industries after 1973. Given the relatively high share of these industries, this significantly affected overall productivity performance. Employment policies of nationalised industries, which are concentrated in the basic metals and chemical sectors, may have played a role (see also below). Productivity growth in all other sectors of industry, although decelerating as in other countries, still compared favourably with developments abroad. In the fabricated metal products, machinery and equipment sectors the productivity growth was exceeded only by Japan.

Another study by the WIFO Institute[8] sheds light on differences in the level of labour productivity between Austria and Germany. In 1964, the Austrian manufacturing sector's output per man-hour was about two-thirds of the German level. In real terms and at current exchange rates, this differential hardly changed until 1980, rising somewhat until 1973 and diminishing thereafter. Between 1964 and 1980 the productivity differentials shrank for fabricated metal products, machinery and equipment, chemicals and non-metallic mineral products but widened for basic metal industries and remained about the same for other sectors. At an average exchange rate over the period of comparison the picture is somewhat more favourable (due to the devaluation of the schilling against the Deutschemark in 1969) and in recent years productivity growth in Germany has tended to be lower than in Austria, although in part for cyclical reasons. But the remaining productivity differential is still important. Available estimates suggest that differences in the capital/labour ratio are by far too small to explain the productivity difference, which means that the Austrian manufacturing sector does not reach the same level of efficiency with about the same quantity of capital. In other words, the quality of productive inputs is lower in Austria than in Germany. The higher share of construction and the lower share of research and development in total manufacturing investment point to a lower quality of capital inputs. Furthermore, given the size structure of enterprises, economies of scale may have been less important in Austria. Also, the qualification level of the Austrian workforce seems to be lower than in Germany[9].

The composition of Austria's foreign trade mirrors the abovementioned structure of output in the manufacturing sector. Austria is a net exporter of basic goods but a net importer

Table 13. **Share of high technology products in exports and imports of manufactures**

Per cent

		1970	1975	1980	1982
United States	Exports	23.4	23.2	15.4	28.3
	Imports	8.5	10.5	13.5	14.5
Japan	Exports	11.6	11.9	15.9	16.5
	Imports	14.7	13.7	13.3	14.8
Germany	Exports	13.6	13.4	14.8	16.0
	Imports	9.9	11.5	13.7	16.5
Netherlands	Exports	12.6	11.8	12.3	11.7
	Imports	12.6	12.3	11.9	12.5
Belgium-Luxembourg	Exports	5.5	7.3	9.0	9.3
	Imports	10.2	11.4	10.1	10.2
Sweden	Exports	10.6	11.6	12.0	12.9
	Imports	12.5	11.8	13.1	14.6
Switzerland	Exports	30.3	28.8	21.4	22.2
	Imports	11.6	12.6	10.7	11.4
Austria	Exports	7.6	7.6	8.9	8.7
	Imports	10.4	11.1	11.9	12.6

Source: OECD Secretariat.

of investment and consumer goods. Compared with other OECD countries Austria's dependence on imported manufactured goods is high, while its export structure is still biased towards basic and semi-finished goods. A recent WIFO study[10] notes an over-representation of "poor-man's" and "every-man's" goods and points out that Austrian exports are still concentrated in product groups where Austria is likely to continue to lose competitiveness against newly-industrialising countries. This particular composition of exports also contributed to a fall in Austria's export price of manufactured goods relative to the average for OECD countries since 1974[11]. Table 13 presents the Austrian performance in high-technology product groups[12] which, in an international setting, should give some indication of Austria's position in advanced technologies. The share of high-technology products in exports of manufactures is still low compared with that of the more advanced OECD economies and its rise over time has been relatively slow. As in many other countries the share of high-technology products in imports is both higher and growing faster than that in exports, but the imbalance is particularly pronounced in Austria. Austria's lagging behind in these rapidly-expanding export markets reflects the relatively small share of chemicals and machinery and equipment in total production and certainly also the relatively low research and development expenditure (see below).

The large share of mass produced goods in Austrian exports and small market shares suggest that exporters are mostly price-takers[13]. This being so, Austrian exporters were unable to pass on fully labour cost increases during most of the 1970s, when wage policies had problems to adjust to the exchange rate target. The effects of the virtually uninterrupted rise in the nominal effective exchange rate on these developments throughout the last decade are hard to judge. In the short run, a revaluation reduces export revenue and profit margins but also the cost of imported goods. Generally lower import price growth will dampen inflation. Finally, lower overall wage increases should stop or reverse the initial profit squeeze at least partially, a process which may take quite a long time as in the case of Austria. Increased competitive pressure from abroad may also be an important incentive to raise efficiency and shift resources away from less profitable activity, thereby contributing to an improvement in the structure and quality of output. On the other hand, however, profits may affect the financial capability of enterprises to adjust.

The export price/unit labour cost ratio, a proxy of profit margins in the exposed sector, fell sharply in the early 1970s (Annex Diagram 1) reflecting the gradual adjustment of the Austrian cost position to the depreciation of the Austrian Schilling in 1969/70. This decline continued until 1977, although on a much smaller scale, mainly as a result of the strong rise of the effective exchange rate in that period. Since then export prices have developed broadly in line with unit labour costs, so that profit margins in the exposed sector have not apparently been squeezed further. This tendency is confirmed by sample data on balance sheets collected by the Nationalbank[14] and the compilation of a cash-flow proxy for industrial enterprises from various sources by WIFO[15]. Apart from cyclical developments, cash-flow as a per cent of gross earnings (turnover less expenditure on goods and material used) has shown a tendency to fall since the early 1960s (Annex Table 3). In the 1970s, the decline was strong between 1974 and 1977 and the following rise was small, so that the cyclical peak values in the late 1970s were considerably below the foregoing in the early 1970s. The data from the balance sheet sample of the Nationalbank (available only from 1973 onwards) confirm the profit squeeze in the second half of the 1970s as shown by the WIFO data. Certainly, this tendency is in line with developments in other countries[16]. A comparison of the cash-flow as a per cent of turnover with developments in Germany, Japan and the United States, nevertheless, suggests that the profit squeeze in Austria may have been more severe up to around 1977 than in other countries[17]. Preliminary estimates, however, point to a marked improvement in profitability in the current upswing, as in other countries. In 1984 the cash-flow ratio was above the long-term average, although the cyclical peak was not yet reached. A breakdown of the WIFO cash-flow data by sectors shows that profit trends were weakest in the basic goods sector (mainly basic metal industries, but also mining) and production of chemicals. The latter was most profitable during the 1950s and in the early 1960s. Profitability in the traditional consumer goods sector has hardly changed since the 1950s, and it has even improved on trend in the production of fabricated metal products, machinery and equipment, although from a relatively low level (Annex Table 3).

Diagram 12. **International comparison of cash-flow and own capital ratios**

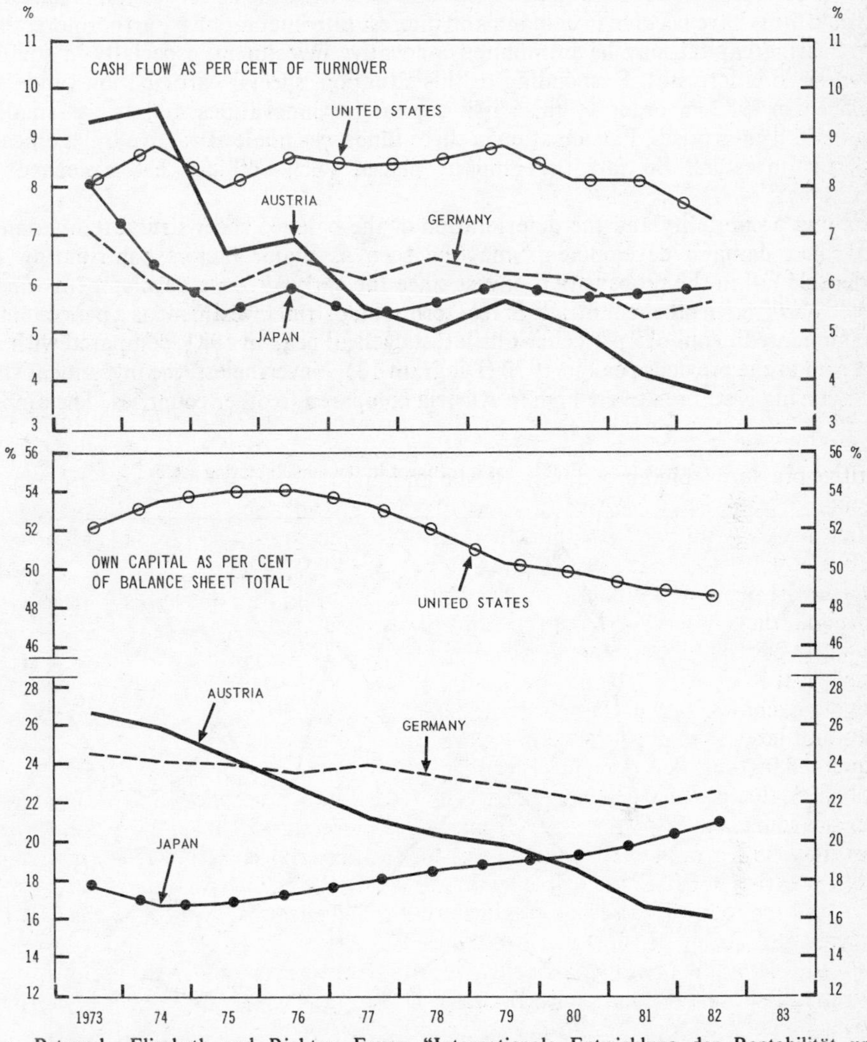

Sources: Petrusch, Elisabeth and Richter, Franz: "Internationale Entwicklung der Rentabilität und der Eigenkapitalentwicklung von Industriebetrieben, verglichen anhand aggregierter Bilanzdaten". In: *Journal für Betriebswirtschaft,* 3/1983, pp. 130-141; and Petrusch, Elisabeth and Richter, Franz: "Erträge bleiben zurück". In: *Industrie,* 42/1984, p. 42.

According to the sample survey of the Nationalbank, own funds (capital plus reserves) as a per cent of the balance sheet total dropped steadily from 26 per cent in 1973 to only 16 per cent in 1982. By international comparison (Diagram 12) the decline was by far the most pronounced. Besides weak profit developments the deterioration of this ratio reflected an underdeveloped equity market. In 1982, there existed only 155 corporate enterprises in the manufacturing sector, and since 1975 new share issues have added only Sch 5.5 billion to capital, compared to an increase in long-term debt of Sch 30 billion. The problems of raising own capital are even worse for private corporations with no access to the stock exchange, for partnerships and for firms organised as sole proprietorship, as a market for participating capital does not exist. The sharp rise in bankruptcies during the last recession illustrates how vulnerable firms have become to demand and interest rate fluctuations. Furthermore, the lack of risk-bearing capital may have inhibited innovative investment, especially in small- and medium-sized enterprises. Responding to this situation, special participation funds[18] were established in 1982 in order to raise risk capital for innovations mainly for small- and medium-sized enterprises. Participation in these funds was made attractive by significant tax credits for investors. So far, the amount placed (Sch 4 billion) has exceeded initial expectations[19].

Falling profitability and the deterioration of the balance sheet structure in connection with weaker demand developments may be seen as major factors contributing to the considerable fall in the propensity to invest since the early 1970s, a development which has also been observed in other countries. In real terms, industrial investment as a per cent of value added amounted to only 15 per cent at its latest cyclical peak in 1981, compared with nearly 20 per cent at the previous peak in 1972 (Diagram 13). Nevertheless, the investment share in manufacturing is still relatively high in Austria compared to other countries. The amount of

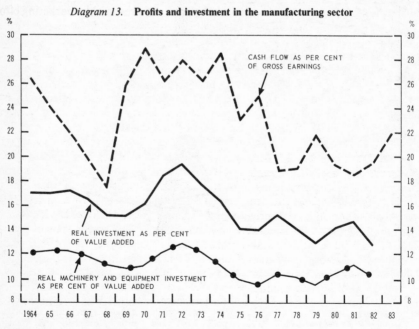

Diagram 13. **Profits and investment in the manufacturing sector**

Sources: WIFO; Austrian Central Statistical Office.

44

real investment did not change much between these two years, while it had risen considerably in the 1960s and early 1970s. Among industrial sectors, investment activity has continued to rise only in the paper, metal products, machinery and equipment-producing industries since 1973, while it has been cut back most in the structurally weak industries (Annex Table 4). Hence, the change in the composition of the capital stock mirrors output developments but the weakening of overall capital formation has led to an ageing of the existing capital stock which slows down trend productivity growth and hinders technical progress. In the current upswing, industrial investment has lagged behind, possibly reflecting a less pronounced improvement of financial conditions than in other sectors of the economy.

The development of an innovatory potential as well as the ability of enterprises to keep up in areas with strong product and process innovation is closely linked to the size of research and development spending. With expenditure of only 0.4 per cent of GDP, Austria was not well placed in this respect in the late 1960s: among OECD countries only a few had a lower ratio[20]. In the 1950s and 1960s this was not felt to be a great problem in Austria as strong productivity growth could be achieved by buying capital equipment and licences abroad[21]. With structural change going in the direction of technology-intensive areas and with increasing government support[22], R&D spending rose rapidly in the 1970s to 0.8 per cent of GDP. This ratio is, however, still among the lower third of OECD countries and seems to have dropped more recently. Besides the structural composition of output (the still relatively small share of chemicals and engineering), the size structure of establishments can partly explain weak R&D spending in Austria. R&D expenditure as a per cent of turnover of small- and medium-sized enterprises is low[23]. Only 3 per cent of enterprises with less than one hundred employees do research compared with 50 per cent of enterprises with more than five hundred employees, the difference in behaviour mainly reflecting economies of scale. But if they do research, small enterprises spend relatively more than larger ones.

The same observation applies to export behaviour and presumably marketing efforts: the number of firms exporting is rising with the size of firms, but export intensity (exports as a per cent of turnover) of exporting firms is not necessarily highest for large firms. Economies of scale in research and development and marketing seem, therefore, to be the two main disadvantages connected with the Austrian size structure of enterprises, which is characterised by a large share of small- and medium-sized enterprises. On the other hand, small- and medium-sized firms are generally assumed to adapt more easily to changes in the economic environment and to be more successful in flexible specialisation, hence playing a more active part in structural adjustment than large units. In fact, as noted above, there is a certain number of small enterprises in Austria actively engaged in research and export activities.

Another characteristic of the Austrian industrial structure is a large share of nationalised industries[24]. After years of favourable relative performance in the early 1970s, nationalised industries have come under strong pressure as the concentration of their activities in structurally weak branches (e.g., iron and steel production) has led to a less favourable development of output than in the private sector (Annex Table 5). Given the location of many enterprises in regions with unfavourable employment prospects and in view of deteriorating overall labour market conditions, labour shedding was kept small until 1980, while it was significant in the private sector (Annex Table 5). The strategy adopted by the authorities was to rationalise the primary products sector but at the same time create employment in high-technology and finished-product areas and industrial services. This policy manifested itself, *inter alia,* in an almost tripling of research and development expenditure since 1974, thirty-five closures, ten mergers and twenty-seven new production lines (e.g., in micro-electronics, numerical machine tools and environmental engineering). The diverging output and employment trends in the nationalised sector nevertheless produced a substantial productivity growth gap, accumulating 35 percentage points in the ten years to 1983 against the industrial average (excluding oil and mining). It is true that this differential also reflects the concentration of nationalised industries in structurally weak sectors. The latters' productivity performance however was also weak by international comparison (see above). The resulting profit squeeze was severe, cash-flow as a per cent of turnover falling from 10 per cent in the early 1970s to 5 per cent in 1979 and only 2 per cent in 1983. Government support became inevitable, particularly in the iron and steel industry, despite cuts in employment since around 1980, and until 1983 Sch 10.5 billion had been paid out to cover losses and facilitate restructuring. In 1983 a further Sch 16.6 billion was granted for restructuring activities in the years to come.

Government support to industrial sectors in difficulty and ailing enterprises has certainly moderated the immediate effects of the adjustment process, which has been especially important in structurally weak regions. It has provided the possibility of revitalising enterprises, re-training of the labour force and introduction of profitable product lines with better demand prospects. Furthermore, potentially achieving lower cost through accelerated labour shedding in nationalised industries would have to be assessed against additional government outlays for unemployment benefits and lower tax receipts. On the other hand, subsidising loss-making enterprises has tied up resources which could have been used for more productive purposes. Given rising budgetary strains and continuing problems in some companies, however, there has been increasing awareness that ailing firms with high levels of employment should not be maintained by government support indefinitely. Employment in nationalised industries has been cut by 9 per cent since 1980. Looking back at developments since the mid-1970s, it is hard to establish a balance between short-run benefits of employment maintenance and restructuring efforts on the one hand and the economic costs of long-term inflexibilities and the foregone gains in efficiency on the other. More recently, government support on top of existing schemes to nationalised industries has been directed to the implementation of plans to phase out obsolete capacity and re-establish financially viable entities by 1986 (except for the iron and steel sector).

Industrial policies influence structural change mainly through various forms of direct and indirect subsidisation. It is difficult to quantify the exact amount of government aid to industry. Table 14 summarises overall trends in subsidisation. Government aid in the form of subsidies and capital transfers more than doubled in the last decade, rising particularly fast at the turn of the 1980s. As a per cent of GDP it reached a peak of 5 per cent in 1981 and seems to have dropped somewhat since then, although the figures for the 1983-85 period may be revised upwards. Since 1978, the Federal Subsidy Report provides an estimate of general government revenue losses through tax reliefs. Including these, government financial aid to enterprises amounted to about 6 percentage points of GDP in 1981-82. The data mentioned, however, are distorted for several reasons: The effects of the accelerated depreciation are calculated on a gross basis, the net effects being lower. On the other hand, part of the aid to nationalised industries (Sch 22 billion since the beginning of the 1980s) is provided in the form of loans taken up by enterprises but repaid by the Government (including interest payments), thereby reducing the amount of subsidisation shown in official statistics in the short run. Furthermore, credits at preferential rates reduce the government's interest income but do not show up as a subsidy or capital transfer in National Accounts statistics.

Government support has been centred on investment activity, being a key factor in fostering industrial growth, structural change and the introduction of new production technologies. Indirect investment promotion comprises accelerated depreciation, investment allowances and the formation of tax-free reserves. For research, environmental protection and

46

Table 14. **Subsidisation by General Government**

Schilling billion; in brackets as per cent of GDP

	1973	1979	1980	1981	1982	1983	1984	1985
Subsidies and capital transfers[1]	24.0	38.8	46.6	52.4	53.0	59.3	60.6	61.6
	(4.4)	(4.2)	(4.6)	(5.0)	(4.7)	(4.9)	(4.7)	(4.5)
of which:								
Subsidies	9.2	26.9	30.1	32.1	34.5	38.7	39.0	39.0
	(1.7)	(2.9)	(3.0)	(3.0)	(3.0)	(3.2)	(3.0)	(2.8)
Subsidies and capital transfers to non-financial enterprises	13.6	36.7	41.7	45.4	48.0	52.6		
	(2.5)	(4.0)	(4.2)	(4.3)	(4.2)	(4.4)		
Tax relief[2]		68.8	74.1	79.9	87.1			
		(7.5)	(7.4)	(7.6)	(7.7)			
of which:								
Non-agricultural enterprises		21.0	22.3	22.7	19.8			
		(2.3)	(2.2)	(2.1)	(1.6)			
Memorandum item:								
Subsidies to manufacturing[1]	4.6	11.6	12.5	14.1	15.6	18.6		
	(0.8)	(1.3)	(1.3)	(1.3)	(1.4)	(1.5)		

1. National Accounts.
2. Federal Subsidy Report, including tax relief to private households.
Sources: Federal Government; Austrian Central Statistical Office; OECD Secretariat.

energy-saving measures, special allowances are granted. All these instruments favour profitable enterprises because they work through a reduction of the tax base. Accelerated depreciation also tended to promote investment in capital-intensive basic goods industries as long as they were profitable and thus was probably a factor behind the maintenance of the relative importance of these industries. As the level of promotion is tied to profit developments it does not favour the foundation of new enterprises. In order to supplement existing tax concessions in a period of low economic growth and depressed profits, a temporary investment premium was introduced in 1982 and has been extended until the end of 1985. For 1984-85 special investment premiums are also granted for the establishment of new businesses in problem areas.

Direct investment promotion comprises a large number of partly overlapping schemes, providing subsidies mainly in the form of low interest loans, interest subsidy schemes and loan guarantees. The institutions responsible for these schemes generally decide on the basis of checklists which investment projects deserve aid. Prominent on these checklists are the creation of new jobs, the promotion of exports, innovation, research and development, energy-saving measures, environmental protection and investment in regions with structural weaknesses. Given the wide range of subsidised activities, it is no wonder that – according to a study of the Nationalbank – about 30 per cent of bank credits to industry are subsidised. In addition to the general schemes, special low-cost financing arrangements are available for specific sectors (e.g. textile industry) and structurally weak regions. Moreover, government support in various forms, including investment grants, was provided to specific projects (e.g. the General Motors plant in Vienna and the cellulose production in Pöls) or enterprises (e.g. as mentioned above in the State-owned sector). Given the large number, overlap and complexity of special support activities their proper economic impact is difficult to assess, but doubts can be cast on the efficiency of the operation of these different schemes. The Government has thus commissioned a comprehensive review of subsidies and transfers in order to increase transparency, evaluate their efficiency and eventually streamline the existing system of subsidisation.

Protectionist barriers at the border and import quotas would seem to be lower than in other countries. Receipts from customs and import duties, as a per cent of imports have come down faster than generally elsewhere and are below the OECD average. The level of protection may be higher than indicated by conventional measures, to the extent that structurally weak industries receive government aid. But since weak industries are also subsidised in other OECD countries, the net effect on relative cost positions is difficult to assess.

V. CONCLUSIONS

Although Austria's economic performance worsened in relation to its own past record, it still compares favourably with that of many Member countries in various respects. Nonetheless, the margin of superiority vis-à-vis the OECD average has been narrowed. Indeed, favourable developments in 1982-83 by European standards owed much to supportive fiscal policy at a time when other countries were trying to correct fiscal imbalances. The move towards fiscal restraint in 1984 was bound to affect demand in that year. But with the damping effect of fiscal measures on domestic demand petering out, the recovery seems to have regained momentum in the second half of 1984 and is expected by the OECD to continue over the next eighteen months. The projected economic expansion should lead to a slight decline in unemployment. The inflation rate is expected to fall and the current account to move towards balance. This projection, however, depends much on a continuing strong rise in exports, a result of both substantial growth of export markets and ongoing improvement of competitiveness under the assumption of constant exchange rates. And the favourable overall picture in the short term conceals some problematic trends which could adversely affect peformance in the medium run.

By international comparison, public debt as a proportion of GDP is still below average and the amount held by foreigners has been reduced. But the rise in the former in the last decade has been more rapid than in the OECD area as a whole. As a result of fiscal measures taken in the mid-1970s public finances have moved into cyclically-adjusted deficit. The latter was substantially reduced in the early 1980s but grew again due to supportive policies thereafter. The restrictive 1984 budget aimed at reversing this trend. But with interest payments and other expenditure items increasing more than revenues, it has become clear that restoration of a sufficient degree of fiscal flexibility necessitates important and often difficult deficit-reducing measures over a longer period of time. The recent pension insurance reform represented a step in the right direction. But, in spite of a rise in contribution rates and some reduction in the growth of benefits, Government transfers will have to cover an increasing share of the pension funds' expenditure in the years to come. The announced tax reform, which would have offered the opportunity to simplify the tax system and review the large number of tax exemptions and allowances, has been postponed. A review of the complex system of subsidisation has only begun. The continuing rapid expansion of off-budget financing, particularly in the form of guaranteed credits, deserves attention, as the final costs to the budget are unclear.

An important element in the strong rise of off-budget financing has been support to nationalised industries. In the nationalised sector, accounting for more than one-fourth of employment in industrial enterprises and including those controlled by nationalised banks, some firms have been facing increasing financial problems, partly because of the concentration of its activities in industries facing slow demand growth and also because of the employment policies pursued up to around 1980. The strategy adopted in the 1970s when structural problems re-emerged was to rationalise the basic goods sector and create employment in high-technology and finished-product areas while at the same time broadly maintaining employment levels in the nationalised industries. This strategy was successfully carried out without special government assistance until the end of the 1970s. It was only in the last few years that the continuing problems in some companies and rising budgetary strains have led to a cut in employment levels in the nationalised sector. Additional government support granted more recently is contingent upon the implementation of plans to phase out obsolete capacities, rationalise existing plants and create new product lines, thus re-establishing financially viable entities in a short period of time. This is a move in a desirable direction suggested by *General Orientations* for positive adjustment agreed by OECD Ministers. But there appears to be much scope for promoting such a policy initiative.

As evidenced by the analysis in Part IV of the Survey, the industrial structure has developed favourably in the long run. As structural change does not, however, seem to have been significantly faster than in other developed countries, relative structural disadvantages have persisted and have become more evident with the slowdown of growth in the world economy. The share of traditional consumer goods industries and basic goods industries in manufacturing has remained high by international comparison. Productivity levels are still considerably below those in many other advanced countries as, for instance, Germany. In order to speed up structural change and increase efficiency the long-term trend of declining profitability and fixed capital formation will have to be reversed. Further action will be needed to promote research and development expenditure and increase the availability of risk capital. It is also important to ensure that sizeable government support to the business sector in various forms of subsidisation, which is intended to provide investment and increase efficiency, does not prove to be counterproductive, lessening incentives for efficiency and delaying the adjustment process. In this respect, although a review is currently under way, lack of transparency in the system of subsidisation makes it difficult to evaluate whether conditions on which government support was granted were met. The current upswing should provide opportunities to cut government assistance where appropriate, in order to reduce imbalances and rigidities and improve the environment for structural change.

The "hard-currency option" imposes considerable self-discipline on trade unions. As implemented in practice it implies that in the medium term unit labour cost developments do not markedly differ from those in Germany. Difficulties to bring incomes policy into line with the exchange rate target contributed to the important imbalance in the current external account in the second half of the 1970s. In the 1983 autumn pay round trade unions abstained from claiming compensation for the inflationary effects of budget consolidation measures, accepting the implicit exchange rate constraint. However, with inflation accelerating markedly, wage settlements in 1984 exceeded considerably those in Germany. In 1985, the inflation rate, although falling, is likely to remain rather higher than in Germany. Austria's competitive position is not, however, expected to deteriorate vis-à-vis the international average. And the current external account position is much better than in the 1970s. However, the danger of external imbalances will necessitate bringing cost and price developments into line with Germany, all the more so if the DM were to strengthen again. In the past Austrian industry coped with foreign trade and exchange rate pressure by adjusting its structure. In a sense, exchange rate developments acted as a stimulant for change. But

49

there is some evidence that since the mid-1970s Austria's capacity for industrial adaptation has been weakened.

Although unemployment is stabilising and remains among the lowest in Member countries, it is much higher than in the 1960s and 1970s and its structural development must be a matter of concern. The unemployment rate for young adults, of minor importance in the past, is rising more than the total and is now above average. Moreover, long-term unemployment as a per cent of the total has sharply increased in the last few years. In the years ahead, some deceleration of potential labour force growth is expected for demographic reasons, but prospects for a significant reduction of the actual unemployment rate are not bright. Relatively satisfactory developments in the recent past owed much to a fall in labour force participation rates. Re-entry into the labour market of the discouraged work force is likely to raise labour supply. Further relief coming from a reduction in the number of foreign workers is also likely to be limited, as it decreased sharply in the last decade. Moreover, rationalisation of industry, though essential for improving the structure over the medium term, will add to the pressure towards higher unemployment. This is another reason for the need to reinforce the policy orientation towards promoting higher growth potential.

In summary, the overall performance has remained satisfactory: the growth rate of GDP, unemployment rates, productivity increases, inflation and the strength of the national currency continue to compare favourably with those in most other European countries. There are, however, areas where medium-term trends demand the attention of the Austrian authorities. Apart from the structural problems in industry, there are certain labour market developments, the inflation rate and problems of public sector finances. The priority given to high employment has helped to keep the unemployment rate relatively low, although it may be asked whether the policy of employment maintenance might not prolong the adjustment process. But, in any case, more attention will have to be paid to the increase in long-term unemployment and to the problems of young people who have completed school or job-training programmes. Furthermore, it will be necessary to lower the inflation rate and speed up structural change so that the movement of unit labour costs does not endanger the external position. Finally, in view of the medium-term trend of the public debt, it would be regrettable if full use were not made of the opportunity provided by the recovery to take further and major steps towards correcting fiscal imbalances.

NOTES AND REFERENCES

1. In National Accounts definition, reflecting *inter alia* sizeable housing loans extended by the States (Länder) recorded below the line of "net lending" as financial transactions.

2. There are various self-administered funds for different professional groups.

3. The introduction of a 7.5 per cent tax on interest income (main exceptions being assets denominated in foreign currency and bonds issued before 1984) reflects budget consolidation efforts. Interest revenues have risen considerably in the last decade. The share of income from property, largely consisting of interest revenues, in private income from property and entrepreneurship, doubled between 1973 and 1983. Although interest income is in principle subject to the progressive income tax, tax evasion is likely to be important, banking practices making control of tax declarations difficult.

4. Koren, Stephan, *Vom Protektionismus zur Integration.* In: Weber, Wilhelm (ed.), *Österreichs Wirtschaftsstruktur,* Wien,"1961, pp. 376-401.

5. WIFO, *Perspektiven der österreichischen Industrie,* Wien, 1982, pp. 162-175.

6. Six indicators are calculated, all based on year-on-year changes of sectoral shares. For example, an indicator is defined as the sum of absolute differences of sector shares between two years $\sum_i /a_{it2}-a_{it1}/$ with a_i's denoting the shares of the different sectors and the t's being time subscripts. Another indicator takes the square root of the sum of squared differences.

7. WIFO, *Situation und Perspektiven der österreichischen Unternehmungen,* Wien, 1983, pp. 12-13.

8. WIFO, *Perspektiven der österreichische Industrie,* Wien, 1982, pp. 77-85.

9. Data for the metal products, machinery and equipment industries, for instance, show that the share of women and foreign workers – mainly used for doing simple work – is higher in Austria than in Germany. Kramer, Helmut: *Industrielle Strukturprobleme Österreichs,* Wien, 1980, pp. 60-64.

10. WIFO, *Perspektiven der österreichischen Industrie,* Wien, 1982, pp. 53-59.

11. Smeral, Egon, *Exportpreise und Exportstruktur.* In: WIFO-Monatsberichte 8/1982, pp. 494-500. According to this study the unfavourable export structure accounts for about half of the decline in relative export prices since 1974.

12. The definition used covers product groups of aerospace industries, automatic data-processing machines and units, electronic equipment and telecommunications, scientific instruments, non-electric machinery and drugs, having been selected on the criterion of a high share of R&D expenditure in output. For further details see: OECD: Trade in high technology products, DSTI/SPR/84.66, DSTI/IND/84.60, Paris, 1984.

13. Smeral, Egon, *Gewinnspannen und Preisverhalten im österreichischen Export.* In: WIFO-Monatsberichte 4/1983, pp. 250-259. An empirical test of the price-taker role shows that export prices in Austria (as well as in, e.g., Belgium or France) are determined by world market prices, the influence of unit labour costs being insignificant. For other countries, e.g., Germany, Switzerland or Sweden, the influence of world market prices is lower and that of unit labour costs significant.

14. For a description see OeNB, *Bilanzkennzahlen österreichischer Industrieunternehmen.* In: Mitteilungen 9/1984, Beilage III.

15. For coverage and definitions see: Hahn, Franz: *Die Entwicklung des industriellen Cash-flows 1983.* In: WIFO-Monatsberichte 10/1983, pp. 648-649.

16. See, e.g., OECD, *Economic Outlook 35,* July 1984, pp. 54-58.

17. The same conclusion is reached by an international comparison of cash-flow/gross earnings ratios in 1973-80: Hahn, Franz: *Die Entwicklung des industriellen Cash-flows 1983.* In: WIFO-Monatsberichte, 10/1983, pp. 655-658.

18. Participation funds have been created mainly by banks. They raise capital in the form of securities and place it by acquiring silent partnerships. As tax credits for investors are conditional on the holding of securities for ten years, a secondary market for these papers has not yet emerged.

19. Projects selected, however, have not always corresponded to the participation funds' purpose as stated by law. A gentlemen's agreement has therefore been concluded between the Finance Ministry and the banks to bring placement policy into line with the intentions of legislation.

20. OECD, *Science resources Newsletter,* 8/1984 and Forschungsförderungsfonds für die gewerbliche Wirtschaft: *Bericht 1984,* Wien, 1984.

21. The coverage ratio (receipts/payments) of the technological balance of payments (money paid or received for the use of patents, licences, trademarks, designs, inventions, etc.) reached only 0.25 per cent in the early 1980s and was below that of Germany (0.5), France (0.9), Japan (0.7), Netherlands (0.7), Sweden (0.9) the United Kingdom (1.2) or the United States (nearly 10.0).

22. Two research funds were founded in 1967. In addition an Innovation Agency has been set up recently, and a programme has been launched to promote the use of micro-electronics, in particular, in small- and medium-sized enterprises (Sch 1 billion in 1985-87).

23. Kager, Marianne and Kepplinger, Hermann: *Forschung und Entwicklung in Österreich,* Wien, 1980, pp. 60-70 and WIFO: *Situation und Perspektiven der österreichischen Unternehmungen,* Wien, 1983, pp. 67-71.

24. In addition to the affiliates of ÖIAG, the State holding company, there are other enterprises controlled by State-owned banks. In 1983, ÖIAG's share in industrial employment was 17 per cent, and employment in enterprises of the State-owned banks adds about 10 percentage points. The analysis refers to the holding alone, but many characteristics listed also apply to the behaviour of State-owned banks' enterprises.

SUPPORTING MATERIAL
ON STRUCTURAL CHANGE IN INDUSTRY

Annex Table 1. **Relative performance of the manufacturing sector**

	1964	1973	1983
	Per cent		
Share in total value added			
(at current prices)			
Primary sector	10.9	7.1	4.5
Secondary sector	45.9	47.0	41.2
of which: Manufacturing	34.3	34.3	29.5
Tertiary sector	43.2	45.9	54.3
Total	100.0	100.0	100.0
	1964-1973	**1973-1983**	**1964-1983**
	Average annual percentage rates of change		
Growth of real valued added			
Primary sector	0.6	2.9	1.8
Secondary sector	6.1	2.1	4.0
of which: Manufacturing	6.2	2.5	4.2
Tertiary sector	4.4	3.8	4.1
Total	4.8	3.0	3.9
	1964-1973	**1973-1982**	**1964-1982**
Growth of employment			
Primary sector	−5.4	−3.1	−4.2
Secondary sector	0.3	−1.1	−0.4
of which: Manufacturing	0.2	−1.0	−0.4
Tertiary sector	1.6	1.9	1.7
Total	−0.1	0.2	0.0

Source: WIFO.

Annex Table 2.   **Foundations and closures of establishments in industry**[1]

	Foundations	Jobs created (thousands)	Closures	Jobs lost (thousands)
1971	235	8.0	114	1.9
1972	279	7.4	245	4.8
1973	205	5.6	206	5.0
1974	220	6.2	218	4.6
1975	154	4.8	247	6.1
1976	179	5.1	242	6.2
1977	185	4.7	192	4.1
1978	188	4.5	252	6.7
1979	246	5.7	168	4.7
1980	201	4.9	133	4.2
1981	201	4.9	204	4.8
1982	160	3.6	262	7.9
1983	152	3.5	224	5.9

1. Excluding handicrafts, including mining.
Sources: WIFO; Austrian Central Statistical Office.

Annex Table 3.   **Cash flow as a per cent of gross earnings in industry**

	Total	Basic industries[1]	Chemicals	Investment goods and technical manufactures[2]	Building materials	Traditional consumer goods[3]
1970	28.8	26.0	30.3	27.8	40.2	37.5
1971	26.2	24.7	31.2	24.9	37.7	26.7
1972	28.0	25.5	29.1	24.6	56.5	33.3
1973	26.3	30.4	26.7	20.0	19.2	22.4
1974	28.6	30.3	36.0	21.9	30.9	22.6
1975	23.0	18.1	39.8	23.6	26.5	28.5
1976	25.0	22.7	28.1	27.5	29.0	26.0
1977	18.9	16.8	9.2	23.2	28.1	27.1
1978	19.1	20.6	4.5	22.5	22.4	15.6
1979	21.8	23.4	16.8	18.6	24.7	25.7
1980[4]	19.4	16.5	11.4	23.1	39.0	27.3
1981[4]	18.6	15.0	6.6	23.7	28.8	24.7
1982[4]	19.5	16.0	17.2	25.9	22.5	28.0
1983[4]	22.0	20.0	20.0	24.5	21.0	29.0
1984[4]	25.0	25.0	25.0	24.0	20.5	29.5
1956/1965	26.3	27.3	32.2	19.8	30.2	25.6
1965/1974	24.7	24.7	28.3	20.2	34.1	25.0
1974/1984	21.9	20.4	19.5	23.5	26.7	25.8

1. Mining, oil, ferrous and non-ferrous metallurgy, foundries, paper.
2. Machinery, vehicles, fabricated metals, electrical industry.
3. Textiles, clothing, paper products, food and drink.
4. WIFO-estimate.
Sources: WIFO.

Annex Table 4.   **Real gross fixed capital formation in manufacturing industry**

	Average annual percentage change			
	1964/1973	1973/1980	1973/1982	1964/1982
Food, beverages and tobacco	1.4	−0.2	−1.1	0.1
Textile, wearing apparel and leather	2.2	−3.3	−4.0	−1.0
Wood and wood products	10.4	−3.3	−4.3	2.8
Paper and paper products	4.4	0.3	1.2	2.0
Chemicals	5.2	2.2	−1.6	1.7
Non-metallic mineral products	4.8	−1.8	−4.2	0.2
Basic metal industries	17.7	−4.2	−4.2	6.2
Fabricated metal products, machinery and equipment	7.8	1.9	1.3	4.5
Total	6.6	−0.5	−1.6	2.5

Source: WIFO.

Annex Table 5.   **State-owned industries' relative economic performance**
Index: 1973 = 100

	1973	1974	1975	1976	1977	1978	1979	1980	1981	1982	1983
Employment											
State-owned industry, total	100	104	103	102	101	99	100	99	96	95[1]	91[1]
Excluding oil and mining	100	104	102	102	101	101	102	101	97	93	89
Total industry	100	100	94	93	94	92	92	93	91	87	83
Production											
State-owned industry, total	100	103	93	97	98	103	109	103	97	94	92
Excluding oil and mining	100	106	100	101	103	109	114	109	106	102	101
Total industry	100	105	97	104	108	111	119	122	120	119	120
Productivity											
State-owned industry, total	100	99	90	95	97	104	109	104	101	99	101
Excluding oil and mining	100	101	98	99	102	108	113	108	108	109	113
Total industry	100	105	103	112	115	120	130	132	132	137	145
Excluding oil and mining	100	106	103	113	116	122	131	134	135	140	148

1.   Estimate.
Sources: Oesterreichische Industrieverwaltungs AG (ÖIAG); Austrian Central Statistical Office.

Annex Diagram 1. Profit indicators

Index, 1970 = 100

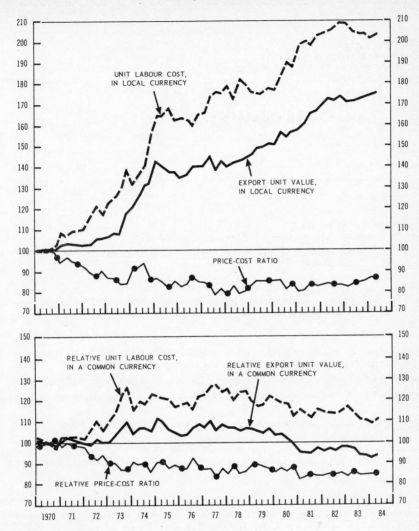

UNIT LABOUR COST, IN LOCAL CURRENCY

EXPORT UNIT VALUE, IN LOCAL CURRENCY

PRICE-COST RATIO

RELATIVE UNIT LABOUR COST, IN A COMMON CURRENCY

RELATIVE EXPORT UNIT VALUE, IN A COMMON CURRENCY

RELATIVE PRICE-COST RATIO

Source: **OECD Secretariat.**

CALENDAR OF MAIN ECONOMIC EVENTS

1983

January

Changes in taxation:

- second step of income tax cuts;
- rise of the investment premium from 6 to 8 per cent up to end-1985.

The interest rate on savings deposits with statutory notice was lowered by ½ percentage point to 4½ per cent.

February

Nationalbank intervened in the money market in the last two weeks in February to keep the money market rate below 6 per cent. Expansive open market operations reached a maximum of Sch 10.5 billion.

March

Nationalbank raised the refinancing quota for credit institutions from 70 to 100 per cent. The 1 per cent extra charge for utilising more than 70 per cent of the ceilings was retained.

Discount and Lombard rates were lowered by 1 percentage point to 3¾ and 4¼ per cent, respectively.

The schilling followed the revaluation of the Deutschemark in the seventh realignment within the European Monetary system.

The unemployment insurance contribution was raised by 1 percentage point to 4 per cent.

June

The interest rate on savings deposits with statutory notice was lowered by ½ percentage point to 4 per cent.

September

The Lombard rate was raised by ½ percentage point to 4¾ per cent. The discount rate was not changed.

The Government announced a budget consolidation package comprising also measures to promote economic growth, employment and environmental protection (for details see draft Budget below).

October

The draft Federal Budget for 1984 (projected net deficit Sch 62.1 billion, 5 per cent of GDP) comprised the following measures expected to raise revenue by Sch 17½ billion and lead to expenditure savings of Sch 10 billion:

- rise in VAT rates by 2 percentage points (7 percentage points in the case of the preferential rate on energy; estimated additional revenue in 1984 Sch 12½ billion, of which Sch 8½ billion going to Federal Government);
- introduction of a (7.5 per cent) tax on interest accruing from schilling deposits (except interest on promoted savings for building purposes; estimated annual receipts Sch 3½ billion from 1985 onwards);
- increase in road transportation contribution, motor vehicle tax, insurance tax and other fiscal charges (Sch 2¼ billion);

- rise in unemployment insurance contributions (by 0.4 percentage points) and pension insurance contributions for self-employed (by 1 percentage point) as well as post and rail charges (Sch 6½ billion);
- abolition of the housing grant (Sch 1¼ billion) and reduction of the childbirth grant (Sch ½ billion);
- economies in social security institutions (Sch 3 billion).

Further measures included:

- foundation of an Environmental Fund (budget cost in 1984 Sch ½ billion);
- foundation of a Recycling Fund;
- interest rate subsidies (2 percentage points for three years for dwelling construction starting in 1984) for building society bridging loans, bonus to building society savers prolonging their contracts;
- foundation of an Innovation Agency;
- extension of the interest rate subsidy scheme for "innovative" investment ("Top-Aktion") to cover a wider range of activities (subsidised credit volume Sch 2 billion in 1984);
- additional promotion of small scale enterprises (Sch ¼ billion);
- abolition of the trading capital tax (Gewerbekapitalsteuer) in three stages, beginning in 1984;
- reduction of the tax on corporate capital by 10 per cent;
- increase in tax allowance for retained earnings for small scale enterprises from 15 to 20 per cent of total profits.

November

Parliament adopted a supplementary Federal Budget for 1983 (Sch 17.6 billion) to cover revenue shortfalls and higher outlays, in particular for social security and labour market promotion.

December

Parliament adopted legislation to promote the construction of 10 000 dwellings.

1984

January

The fiscal measures announced in September 1983 and comprised in the draft Federal Budget of October 1983 became effective.

The Federal Government adopted measures to promote economic growth and structural change, comprising the promotion of the use of micro-electronics and a special grant for investment in structurally weak regions.

March

Parliament passed legislation introducing a 40 per cent premium on machinery and equipment investment in structurally weak regions in 1984 and 1985.

The discount rate was raised by ½ percentage point to 4¼ per cent and the Lombard rate by ¾ percentage points to 5½ per cent.

Nationalbank used foreign exchange swap operations to reduce liquidity pressure in the money market until early May 1984.

June

The Federal Government announced changes in public pension schemes, to take effect in January 1985. Major measures comprise a rise in contribution rates by ½ percentage point for both employees and employers in 1985 as well as changes in the computation of pensions and pension increases from 1986 onwards.

The Federal Government announced a subsidy scheme (Sch 1 billion from 1985 to 1987) promoting research in and application of micro-electronics.

The discount rate was raised by ¼ percentage point to 4½ per cent.

September

Negotiations between the Federal Government and local governments resulted in a redistribution of fiscal revenues in favour of States (Länder) and municipalities.

October

The draft Federal Budget for 1985 (projected net deficit Sch 60½ billion, 4½ per cent of GDP) and related legislation comprised the following measures:

- increase in family allowances (additional expenditure Sch 2 billion);
- reduction of the tax rate on interest revenue from 7½ to 5 per cent;
- grant of 12 per cent for investment outlays on environmental protection;
- rise in pension insurance contributions and shifts of funds between social security institutions (Budget savings in 1985 Sch 6½ billion).

STATISTICAL ANNEX

Table A. **Gross domestic product**
Sch. billion

	1979	1980	1981	1982	1983	1979	1980	1981	1982	1983
	Current prices					1976 prices				
Expenditure:										
Private consumption	511.7	552.5	595.6	642.9	696.4	446.0	452.6	453.9	460.5	483.6
Public consumption	166.0	178.7	195.2	214.3	226.0	141.9	145.5	148.3	151.7	154.7
Gross domestic fixed capital formation	230.9	254.1	266.5	262.8	267.2	197.9	205.1	200.8	187.2	183.7
Construction[1]	125.9	135.0	142.0	141.4	145.8	104.3	103.5	100.8	94.2	93.7
Machinery and equipment[1]	92.8	106.0	110.6	107.4	107.4	83.4	91.3	90.1	83.6	80.9
Change of stocks, incl. statistical errors	13.9	28.8	12.9	-0.7	6.6	14.7	22.4	3.8	-0.2	5.0
Exports of goods and services	344.9	388.3	434.0	463.3	495.4	305.7	325.9	342.5	350.0	371.5
less: Imports of goods and services	348.8	407.7	448.0	444.5	485.8	310.2	331.4	330.5	321.9	353.7
Gross domestic product at market prices	918.5	994.7	1 056.3	1 138.1	1 205.8	796.1	820.0	818.9	827.2	844.7
Origin by sector:										
Agriculture, forestry and fishing	40.3	44.3	43.4	43.5	44.3	38.1	39.7	37.8	43.2	42.0
Manufacturing and mining	264.9	281.4	293.9	314.1	327.0	241.2	248.4	246.6	246.5	250.9
Construction	75.3	81.2	84.8	86.6	88.3	61.0	61.2	58.6	56.3	55.7
Other	538.0	587.8	634.2	693.9	746.2	455.8	470.7	475.9	481.2	496.1
	Current prices					Current prices percentage distribution				
Distribution of the national income:										
Compensation of employees	504.5	545.6	589.5	617.7	643.9	74.0	74.0	75.9	73.7	72.8
Income from property and entrepreneurship	195.4	209.7	207.2	247.2	270.1	28.6	28.4	26.7	29.5	30.5
Savings of corporations										
Direct taxes on corporations										
Government income from property and entrepreneurship	13.2	18.5	22.4	22.7	22.2	1.9	2.5	2.9	2.7	2.5
less: Interest on public debt and consumer debt	31.0	36.4	42.5	49.1	51.3	4.5	4.9	5.5	5.9	5.8
National income	682.2	737.5	776.6	838.4	885.0	100.0	100.0	100.0	100.0	100.0

1. Excluding VAT.
Source: Österreichisches Institut für Wirtschaftsforschung.

Table B. **General government income and expenditure**

Sch. billion

	1976	1977	1978	1979	1980	1981	1982	1983
Operating surplus and property income receivable	10.2	10.3	12.2	13.2	18.5	22.4	22.7	22.2
Casualty insurance claims receivable	0.1	0.1	0.2	0.2	0.2	0.2	0.2	0.2
Indirect taxes	119.5	135.9	139.3	151.2	162.8	174.4	185.0	200.0
Direct taxes	82.8	93.7	110.8	118.0	128.4	144.2	149.5	156.6
Compulsory fees, fines, and penalties	1.6	2.5	2.6	2.7	2.9	3.4	3.4	3.6
Social security contributions	75.4	86.6	102.9	112.1	124.6	135.6	141.3	147.4
Unfunded employee welfare contributions imputed	17.2	18.6	20.7	22.3	23.7	25.9	28.7	31.1
Current transfers n.e.c. received from the rest of the world	0.6	0.6	0.6	0.6	0.6	0.5	0.6	0.7
Current receipts	307.4	348.2	389.2	420.4	461.6	506.6	531.5	561.8
Final consumption expenditure	127.8	138.7	154.1	166.0	178.7	195.2	214.3	226.0
Property income payable	12.2	14.8	18.7	21.3	24.7	29.3	35.2	37.3
Net casualty insurance premiums payable	0.1	0.1	0.2	0.2	0.2	0.2	0.2	0.2
Subsidies	20.8	23.3	26.5	26.9	30.0	32.1	34.5	38.7
Social security benefits and social assistance grants	64.7	71.6	78.8	86.7	94.5	103.4	112.6	122.0
Current transfers to priv. non-profit inst. serving households	36.0	40.9	50.9	54.5	56.2	60.1	67.0	71.1
Unfunded employee welfare benefits	27.6	30.0	33.6	36.0	38.6	42.3	46.1	49.7
Current transfers n.e.c. paid to the rest of the world	1.7	1.9	2.2	2.4	2.5	2.7	3.0	3.3
Current disbursements	291.0	321.4	365.0	393.9	425.5	465.2	513.0	548.3
Saving	16.4	26.8	24.2	26.5	36.2	41.3	18.5	13.6
Consumption of fixed capital	5.3	5.8	6.3	6.8	7.5	8.3	9.1	9.9
Capital transfers received, net, from	-12.4	-11.7	-12.1	-11.8	-16.5	-20.3	-18.5	-20.6
Other resident sectors	-12.3	-11.6	-12.0	-11.7	-16.4	-20.2	-18.4	-20.5
The rest of the world	-0.1	-0.1	-0.1	-0.1	-0.1	-0.1	-0.1	-0.1
Finance of gross accumulation	9.4	20.9	18.4	21.4	27.2	29.4	9.1	2.8
Gross capital formation	33.7	36.8	38.8	40.2	41.6	43.8	42.6	41.4
Purchases of land, net	2.8	2.9	2.9	3.1	2.6	1.9	1.8	2.1
Net lending	-27.1	-18.8	-23.3	-22.0	-17.0	-16.4	-35.3	-40.7

Source: Bundesministerium für Finanzen.

Table C. **Output, employment, wages and productivity in industry**

	1980	1981	1982	1983	1983 Q1	Q2	Q3	Q4	1984 Q1	Q2	Q3
Output in industry, seasonally adjusted (1980 = 100):											
Total industry	100.0	98.4	97.6	98.5	95.7	98.6	100.3	99.6	101.7	102.2	105.2
Mining	100.0	103.3	107.7	106.1	104.6	107.1	108.3	104.9	113.4	110.7	111.0
Manufacturing	100.0	97.5	96.4	97.6	94.2	97.4	99.9	99.0	101.6	102.0	105.6
Basic metals	100.0	95.9	91.1	96.0	89.7	94.4	98.4	101.6	104.9	100.1	105.1
Metal products, machinery, and equipment	100.0	96.8	99.7	99.5	96.1	100.5	101.6	99.7	102.8	100.0	104.0
Food, beverages, tobacco	100.0	97.8	99.6	100.2	101.2	99.4	101.3	99.2	99.3	101.0	100.6
Textiles, clothing, and leather	100.0	99.4	94.4	91.1	87.0	91.3	91.7	94.3	95.1	91.9	93.7
Chemicals	100.0	95.8	92.6	96.5	91.2	93.9	100.0	101.4	103.1	110.6	112.0
Employment:											
Not seasonally adjusted ('000)	627	614	589	565	565	563	567	565	558	558	565
Wages and productivity:											
Gross hourly earnings for wage earners (schillings)	73	78	83	87	76	92	80	99	78	96	83
Gross monthly earnings, employees (schillings)	14 624	15 769	16 869	17 740	15 250	18 819	16 509	20 382	16 061	19 739	17 157
Output per hour (1970 = 100)	177.7	179.0	186.6	198.6	183.7	200.7	203.5	206.3	195.1	210.5	212.0
Wages and salaries per unit of output (1970 = 100)	184.2	199.1	205.9	204.9	188.6	214.2	193.2	223.5	179.0	215.8	193.0

Source: Österreichisches Institut für Wirtschaftsforschung.

Table D. **Retail sales and prices**
(1980 = 100)

	1979	1980	1981	1982	1983	1983 Q1	1983 Q2	1983 Q3	1983 Q4	1984 Q1	1984 Q2	1984 Q3
Retail sales												
Total	93.3	100.0	106.3	112.1	120.8	105.0	114.5	116.7	146.9	107.0	119.0	119.0
of which: Durables	94.0	100.0	101.1	106.2	123.4	105.5	118.5	112.9	156.9	96.9	115.6	110.4
Prices:												
Consumer prices												
Total	94.0	100.0	106.8	112.6	116.3	115.2	115.4	116.8	118.0	121.8	122.4	123.4
Food	95.7	100.0	105.9	110.6	113.4	112.3	112.4	114.1	114.7	119.0	119.9	120.6
Rent	95.6	100.0	106.4	116.2	127.1	123.4	125.8	128.3	130.5	132.9	133.9	137.5
Other goods and services	93.1	100.0	107.3	113.1	116.6	115.7	115.7	116.8	118.2	121.9	122.3	123.3
Wholesale prices												
Total	92.1	100.0	108.1	111.5	112.1	112.3	112.0	111.4	113.0	116.4	117.3	115.5
Agricultural goods	91.9	100.0	108.2	108.7	108.5	109.9	113.3	104.5	106.3	118.0	122.0	107.0
Food	97.6	100.0	103.0	108.4	111.2	110.3	110.4	111.0	112.9	115.3	116.7	118.0
Cost of construction (residential)	92.8	100.0	108.3	115.3	119.5	117.6	119.9	120.4	119.5	122.3	124.1	124.1

Source: Österreichisches Institut für Wirtschaftsforschung.

63

Table E. Money and banking[1]
End of period

	1981	1982	1982 Q4	1983 Q1	Q2	Q3	Q4	1984 Q1	Q2	Q3
Interest rates (per cent):										
Discount rate	6.75	4.75	4.75	3.75	3.75	3.75	3.75	4.25	4.50	4.50
Average bond yield[2]	10.71	9.01	9.01	8.22	8.08	8.22	8.07	7.90	7.96	8.05
Money circulation external reserves (Sch. bill.):										
Notes and coin in circulation	96.0	100.3	100.3	101.8	107.9	109.6	109.9	105.1	110.4	109.9
Sight liabilities of the Central Bank	45.5	46.1	46.1	43.9	43.5	42.3	46.9	47.7	49.0	45.4
Gross external reserves of the Central Bank	115.5	118.7	118.7	115.0	112.1	115.4	114.2	117.5	112.5	111.6
of which: Gold	39.4	39.4	39.4	39.4	39.4	39.4	39.4	39.4	39.4	39.4
Credit institutions (Sch. bill.):										
Credits to domestic non-banks	867.6	934.7	934.7	936.7	960.8	974.1	1000.9	1002.8	1040.4	1063.6
Short-term	233.1	248.5	248.5		252.9	255.9	268.8	261.3	268.7	276.0
Medium-term (1 to 5 years)	156.7	158.2	158.2		158.7	157.7	159.0	153.1	157.6	162.2
Long-term	447.8	528.0	528.0		549.1	560.4	573.1	588.5	614.1	625.4
Deposits from domestic non-banks	785.0	879.2	879.2	882.3	896.9	914.9	928.3	928.9	947.5	957.0
Sight	76.7	87.7	87.7	84.5	96.8	97.5	97.8	91.2	104.0	100.9
Time[3]	89.4	98.5	98.5	102.0	102.7	115.5	109.9	110.2	112.6	120.8
Savings	618.9	693.0	693.0	695.8	697.4	701.9	720.6	727.5	730.9	735.2
Holdings of domestic Treasury bills	27.8	40.9	40.9	42.3	45.9	47.0	45.1	44.1	47.3	47.3
Holdings of other domestic securities	182.6	200.8	200.8	205.2	215.2	219.1	224.4	219.0	221.5	220.6
Foreign assets	382.7	454.1	454.1	455.4	502.2	525.5	542.9	558.9	570.6	631.8
Foreign liabilities	436.3	478.8	478.8	468.6	518.1	529.2	559.5	571.6	589.1	646.0

1. Totals may not add due to rounding.
2. Average effective yields on circulating issues.
3. Including funded borrowing of banks.
Sources: Österreichisches Nationalbank; Österreichische Länderbank.

64

Table F. The Federal budget
National accounts basis
Sch. billion

				Outturn			
	1978	1979	1980	1981	1982	1983[1]	1984[2]
1. Current revenue	187.9	207.2	223.8	247.3	256.2	272.2	302.9
Direct taxes of households	55.1	58.4	63.0	71.4	75.1	78.8	85.7
Indirect taxes	96.4	106.6	113.1	122.5	127.1	136.9	158.1
Corporate taxes	11.7	13.3	14.3	14.8	13.5	14.3	14.9
Income from property and entrepreneurship	8.9	9.8	12.5	15.8	15.0	15.6	15.9
Current transfers from abroad	0.5	0.4	0.4	0.3	0.3	0.3	0.5
Other	15.3	18.7	20.5	22.5	25.2	26.3	27.8
2. Current expenditure	197.1	212.9	222.2	242.0	275.3	301.1	324.5
Goods and services	56.0	59.8	63.4	69.7	78.5	82.7	87.5
Subsidies	19.2	20.0	21.1	22.9	26.3	30.1	33.0
Public debt	13.3	15.4	17.6	20.6	25.3	26.8	32.5
Transfers to abroad	0.6	0.6	0.7	0.8	0.9	0.9	2.3
Transfers to public authorities	44.7	49.6	50.1	54.2	62.8	74.1	76.0
Transfers to private households	42.2	44.6	45.0	47.4	52.8	55.6	60.5
Other	21.1	22.9	24.3	26.4	28.7	30.9	32.7
3. Net public savings (1 – 2)	–9.5	–5.8	1.6	5.0	–19.2	–28.9	–21.6
4. Depreciation	1.3	1.4	1.5	1.7	1.8	2.0	2.2
5. Gross savings (3 + 4)	–8.2	–4.4	3.1	6.7	–17.4	–26.9	–19.4
6. Gross asset formation	11.0	12.8	14.7	14.9	13.3	13.7	15.1
7. Balance of income effective transactions (5 – 6)	–19.2	–17.2	–11.6	–8.2	–30.7	–40.6	–34.5
8. Capital transfers (net)	10.9	10.8	13.9	16.3	15.0	17.9	19.1
9. Financial balance (7 – 8)	–30.2	–28.0	–25.5	–24.3	–45.6	–58.5	–53.6

1. Preliminary.
2. Estimated outcome.
Sources: Österreichisches Statistisches Zentralamt; Ministry of Finance; Österreichisches Institut für Wirtschaftsforschung.

Table G. Balance of payments
Sch. million

	1972	1973	1974	1975	1976	1977	1978	1979	1980	1981	1982	1983
Trade balance[1]	−30 865	−33 766	−32 271	−30 629	−52 516	−71 296	−50 675	−58 658	−87 483	−77 130	−62 613	−70 753
Exports	94 776	113 853	156 266	145 576	168 890	180 634	194 073	227 474	247 787	284 659	298 930	333 485
Imports	125 641	147 619	188 536	176 205	221 406	251 930	244 748	286 132	335 270	361 789	361 543	404 238
Services, net	27 198	28 198	26 445	27 620	28 053	24 414	30 465	34 855	42 159	41 393	46 158	40 434
Foreign travel, net	27 668	29 609	26 147	29 527	29 208	27 254	32 931	35 373	42 938	46 398	49 234	42 334
Receipts	38 826	42 895	42 773	48 450	56 437	61 958	68 551	75 010	83 363	90 952	95 031	94 386
Expenditure	11 158	13 286	16 626	18 922	27 228	34 704	35 620	39 636	40 424	44 554	45 797	52 052
Investment income, net	−1 934	−2 567	−1 947	−2 390	−3 847	−5 572	−7 071	−6 442	−6 838	−7 442	−6 962	−6 696
Other services, net	1 464	1 156	2 245	483	2 692	2 732	4 605	5 924	6 059	2 437	3 886	4 796
Unclassified goods and services	994	1 848	100	2 264	7 472	13 921	11 129	9 319	25 093	15 692	29 877	35 777
Transfers, net	−801	−1 604	−2 978	−2 601	−1 910	−2 322	−130	387	−1 144	−1 362	−1 238	−1 455
Public	−112	−103	−194	−39	−194	−285	−160	−312	−399	−471	−608	−792
Private	−689	−1 501	−2 784	−2 562	−1 716	−2 037	30	699	−745	−892	−630	−664
Current balance	−3 474	−5 724	−8 704	−3 346	−18 901	−35 283	−9 211	−14 098	−21 376	−21 408	12 184	4 003
Long-term capital, net	1 896	−3 752	7 378	18 214	−1 261	9 828	20 430	−7 172	7 084	15 040	−9 864	−24 054
Official[2]	−2 262	−1 193	2 680	15 985	3 245	12 048	12 221	2 170	5 938	12 281	14 176	6 428
Private	4 158	−2 559	4 698	2 228	−4 506	−2 220	8 209	−9 342	1 145	2 759	−24 040	−30 482
Basic balance	−1 578	−9 476	−1 326	14 868	−20 162	−25 455	11 219	−21 270	−14 292	−6 368	2 320	−20 051
Non-monetary short-term capital	−72	697	−448	8	−737	5 673	−371	−4 012	−5 209	2 003	−6 261	−2 651
Errors and omissions	4 103	3 714	2 799	2 977	2 587	1 147	3 084	1 013	2 865	4 508	10 623	−6 974
Balance on non-monetary transactions	2 453	−5 065	1 025	17 853	−18 312	−18 635	13 932	−24 269	−16 636	143	6 682	−29 676
Private monetary institutions' short-term capital	5 590	881	4 944	2 592	14 997	11 628	3 227	7 256	38 313	7 985	−2 939	21 832
Balance on official settlements excluding allocation of SDRs, monetization of gold and revaluation of reserve currencies	8 043	−4 184	5 969	20 445	−3 315	−7 007	17 159	−17 013	21 677	8 127	3 743	−7 844
Gold	24	23	0	0	1	99	11 443	9 930	1	0	14	17

Changes in reserves arising from allocation of SDRs, monetization of gold and revaluation of reserve currencies	532	−1 316	−2 089	2 213	−3 554	−2 160	9 278	7 935	4 413	3 974	803	6 519
Allocation of SDRs	708	0	0	0	0	0	0	598	560	597	0	0
Changes in total reserves	8 575	−5 100	3 879	22 659	−6 869	−9 167	26 438	−9 078	26 090	12 102	4 546	−1 326
Conversion factor (Sch. per dollar)	23.12	19.59	18.69	17.42	17.94	16.53	14.52	13.37	12.94	15.92	17.06	17.97

1. Including non monetary gold and adjustments to trade according to foreign trade statistics.
2. Including Central Bank.
Source: Österreichische Nationalbank.

Table H. **Merchandise trade by commodity group and area**
Sch. billion

	Imports					Exports				
	1979	1980	1981	1982	1983	1979	1980	1981	1982	1983
Total	269.9	315.8	334.5	332.6	348.3	206.3	226.2	251.8	266.9	277.1
By commodity group:										
Food, drink, tobacco	17.2	18.8	20.4	20.8	21.4	8.1	9.2	10.8	12.1	12.3
Raw materials	20.0	22.4	23.7	23.2	21.0	17.4	20.1	19.6	17.7	18.2
Mineral fuels, energy	33.4	48.9	62.4	53.7	48.1	3.0	3.6	4.4	4.1	4.0
Chemicals	26.5	29.2	30.7	33.1	35.0	17.5	20.0	23.3	24.1	25.9
Machinery and transport equipment	80.1	90.4	91.5	92.4	103.6	58.2	62.6	69.0	78.7	83.6
Other	92.7	106.1	105.8	109.4	119.2	102.1	110.7	124.7	130.2	133.1
By area:										
OECD countries	215.2	244.6	250.0	255.3	274.1	149.3	164.2	177.3	189.3	198.6
EEC countries[1]	174.7	197.2	197.1	203.4	218.4	110.4	124.8	133.0	141.6	148.8
Germany	114.2	128.9	130.0	134.9	144.6	62.5	70.0	73.3	78.3	85.3
Italy	25.1	28.7	27.9	28.7	31.0	20.2	24.8	25.3	24.2	24.6
France	11.0	12.5	12.5	12.9	14.3	6.6	7.8	9.0	11.3	10.4
UK	7.9	8.7	7.8	7.3	7.5	9.2	8.3	10.5	11.5	11.3
EFTA countries[2]	22.6	24.9	25.4	25.6	27.2	25.2	28.1	30.4	31.2	29.7
Switzerland	14.5	15.8	16.0	15.9	16.5	15.2	17.0	18.6	18.7	18.9
USA	8.5	10.7	13.7	12.5	11.7	5.2	4.9	6.5	7.8	8.2
Other OECD countries	9.4	11.8	13.8	13.8	16.8	8.5	6.4	7.4	8.7	11.9
Non-OECD countries	54.7	71.2	84.5	77.3	74.2	57.0	62.0	74.5	77.6	78.5
Eastern Europe[3]	23.7	30.7	39.8	36.9	36.5	26.6	27.3	28.7	29.6	33.5
Africa	7.8	10.5	12.5	12.5	12.0	8.0	10.2	14.4	13.7	11.4
Latin America	5.4	6.0	5.3	6.7	8.0	2.8	3.3	4.3	3.4	2.9
Far and Middle East	15.3	21.2	24.1	17.9	14.0	11.1	13.5	18.8	22.6	23.1
Other	2.5	2.8	2.8	3.3	3.7	8.5	7.7	8.3	8.3	7.6
Index, in real terms (1979 = 100)	100	106	102	101	107	100	105	110	111	116
Index of average value (1979 = 100)	100	111	122	123	121	100	105	111	116	116

1. From 1980 including Greece.
2. Including Finland.
3. Excluding Yugoslavia.
Source: Österreichisches Institut für Wirtschaftsforschung.

BASIC STATISTICS :

INTERNATIONAL COMPARISONS

		Reference period	Units
POPULATION	Total	Mid-1981	Thousands
	Inhabitants per sq. km of land area	»	Number
	Net average annual increase	Mid-1971 to Mid-1981	%
EMPLOYMENT	Total civilian	1981	Thousands
	of which: Agriculture	»	% of total
	Industry[4]	»	»
	Other	»	»
GROSS DOMESTIC PRODUCT in purchasers' values		1981	US $ billion[11]
Average annual volume growth[6]		1976 to 1981	%
Per capita		1981	US $[11]
GROSS FIXED CAPITAL FORMATION		1981	% of GDP
of which: Transport, machinery and equipment		»	»
Residential construction		»	»
Average annual volume growth[6]		1976 to 1981	%
GROSS SAVING RATIO[12]		1981	% of GDP
GENERAL GOVERNMENT			
Current expenditure on goods and services		1981	% of GDP
Current disbursements[13]		»	»
Current receipts		»	»
NET OFFICIAL DEVELOPMENT ASSISTANCE		1982	% of GNP
INDICATORS OF LIVING STANDARDS			
Private consumption per capita		1981	US $[11]
Passenger cars, per 1 000 inhabitants		1978	Number
Telephones, per 1 000 inhabitants		1981	»
Television sets, per 1 000 inhabitants		1980	»
Doctors, per 1 000 inhabitants		1981	%
Full-time school enrolment[15]		1980	%
Infant mortality[17]		1982	Number
WAGES AND PRICES		Average annual increase	
Hourly earnings in manufacturing		1977 to 1982	%
Consumer prices		»	%
FOREIGN TRADE			
Exports of goods, fob		1982	US $ million[11]
As percentage of GDP		»	%
Average annual volume increase		1977 to 1982	%
Imports of goods, cif		1982	US $ million[11]
As percentage of GDP		»	%
Average annual volume increase		1977 to 1982	%
TOTAL OFFICIAL RESERVES[24]		Mid-1982	US $ million
As ratio of average monthly imports of goods		In 1982	ratio

1. Partly from national sources.
2. Total resident population.
3. Private and socialised sector.
4. According to the definition used in OECD: Labour Force Statistics: mining, manufacturing, construction and utilities (electricity, gas and water).
5. Social product.
6. At constant prices.
7. Including Luxembourg.
8. Excluding ships operating overseas.
9. Fiscal year beginning 1st April.
10. Fiscal year beginning 1st July.

ugal	Spain	Sweden	Switzer-land	Turkey	United Kingdom	United States	Yugo-slavia[1]
﹝0	37 654	8 324	6 429	45 747	56 020	229 849	22 520
8	75	19	156	59	230	25	87
1	1.0	0.3	0.2	2.3	0.1	1.0	0.9
θ	10 931	4 225	3 054	14 668	23 819	100 397	9 690[3]
7	18.2	5.6	7.0	60.1	2.6	3.5	33.8
5	35.2	31.3	39.3	16.4	35.7	30.1	22.3
8	46.6	63.1	53.7	23.5	61.7	66.4	41.9
18	186.1	122.4	94.5	57.6	497.8	2 906.3	67.8[26]
0	1.4	1.0	2.4	2.0	0.5	2.8	..
1(8	4 938	13 505	14 778	1 262	8 886	12 647	3 034[26]
3	20.1	19.3	24.2	19.9	15.9	17.9	31.0[26]
8	6.5[26]	7.8	7.6	8.7[22]	8.1	8.1	..
8	5.5[23]	4.6	16.6	2.7[22]	2.1	3.6	7.2[26]
6	—1.2	—1.4	5.1	—2.4	—1.9	3.3	5.7[26]
7	18.0	16.0	28.7	20.3	17.3	18.9	37.0[26]
9	11.8	29.3	12.5	12.6	22.3	18.1	16.9[26]
9[14]	29.4[26]	60.3	28.1	..	44.6	34.2	..
1[14]	30.0[26]	59.0	32.6	..	43.4	33.7	..
	..	1.02	0.25	..	0.38	0.27	..
﹝8	3 449	7 091	9 244	885	5 382	8 085	1 580[26]
8	178	345	324	14	262	526	85
9	329	828	751	39[23]	507	789	71[22]
1	252	381[29]	314[29]	75[29]	404	624	192[29]
,9[26]	2.6	2.2[26]	1.6	0.6	1.3	2.0[26]	1.3[22]
5[22]	87[23]	86	..	37[23]	82[23]	100[30]	83
0[26]	10.3[28]	6.8	7.6[28]	131.0[27]	11.8[28]	11.2	30.7[28]
3	20.5	8.7	4.4	..	13.4	8.4	25.4
0	16.0	10.3	4.2	56.5	12.0	9.8	27.3
2﹝6	20 568	26 736	25 932	5 772	97 224	212 280	8 364
12	11.48	27.31	27.04	10.99	20.63	7.02	13.46[28]
	7.57[33]	3.52	1.85	14.25	1.55	2.91	..
240	31 620	27 624	28 596	8 940	99 672	243 948	10 980
13	17.65	28.22	29.82	17.63	21.15	8.06	17.67[28]
	2.06[33]	1.89	4.43	—4.39	3.32	—0.31	..
44	9 809	3 798	18 024	1 254	14 572	27 710	1 260
'5	3.72	1.65	7.56	1.68	1.76	1.36	1.38

30. Primary and secondary schools.
31. 1976 to 1981.
32. 1977 to 1980.
33. 1977 to 1979.
Note: Figures within brackets are estimates by the OECD Secretariat.
Sources: Common to all subjects and countries: OECD: *Labour Force Statistics, Main Economic Indicators, National Accounts, Observer, Statistics of Foreign Trade (Series A)*; Statistical Office of the European Communities, *Basic Statistics of the Community;* IMF, *International Financial Statistics;* UN, *Statistical Yearbook.*
National sources have also been used when data are not available according to standard international definitions.

EMPLOYMENT OPPORTUNITIES

Economics and Statistics Department

OECD

A. **Administrator.** A number of economist positions may become available in 1985 in areas such as monetary and fiscal policy, balance of payments, resource allocation, macroeconomic policy issues, short-term forecasting and country studies. *Essential* qualifications and experience: advanced university degree in economics; good knowledge of statistical methods and applied econometrics; two or three years experience in applied economic analysis; command of one of the two official languages (English and French). *Desirable* qualifications and experience also include: familiarity with the economic problems and data sources of a number of Member countries; proven drafting ability; experience with the estimation, simulation and implementation of computer-based economic models; some knowledge of the other official language.

B. **Principal Administrator.** A number of senior economist positions may become available in 1985 in areas such as monetary and fiscal policy, balance of payments, resource allocation, macroeconomic policy issues, short-term forecasting and country studies. *Essential* qualifications and experience: advanced university degree in economics; extensive experience in applied economic analysis, preferably with a central bank, economics/finance ministry or institute of economic research; good knowledge of statistical methods and applied econometrics; command of one of the two official languages (English and French) and proven drafting ability. *Desirable* qualifications and experience also include: experience in using economic analysis for formulating policy advice; familiarity with a number of OECD economies; experience in using economic analysis economic models; good knowledge of the other official language.

These positions carry a basic slary (tax free) from FF 165 760 or FF 204 511 (Administrator) and from FF 234 430 (Principal Administrator). Staff who are neither French nationals nor permanently resident in France before joining OECD receive an expatriation allowance of 16 per cent of basic salary, supplemented by further additional allowances depending on family and residence situation.

Initial appointment will be on a two three year fixed-term contract.

Vacancies are open to both male and female candidtates from OECD Member countries. Applications citing reference "ECSUR", together with a detailed curriculum vitæ in English or French, should be sent to:

Head of Personnel
OECD
2, rue André-Pascal
75775 PARIS CEDEX 16
France

OECD SALES AGENTS
DÉPOSITAIRES DES PUBLICATIONS DE L'OCDE

ARGENTINA – ARGENTINE
Carlos Hirsch S.R.L., Florida 165, 4° Piso (Galería Guemes)
1333 BUENOS AIRES, Tel. 33.1787.2391 y 30.7122

AUSTRALIA – AUSTRALIE
Australia and New Zealand Book Company Pty, Ltd.,
10 Aquatic Drive, Frenchs Forest, N.S.W. 2086
P.O. Box 459, BROOKVALE, N.S.W. 2100. Tel. (02) 452.44.11

AUSTRIA – AUTRICHE
OECD Publications and Information Center
4 Simrockstrasse 5300 Bonn (Germany). Tel. (0228) 21.60.45
Local Agent/Agent local :
Gerold and Co., Graben 31, WIEN 1. Tel. 52.22.35

BELGIUM – BELGIQUE
Jean De Lannoy, Service Publications OCDE
avenue du Roi 202, B-1060 BRUXELLES. Tel. 02/538.51.69

CANADA
Renouf Publishing Company Limited,
Central Distribution Centre,
61 Sparks Street (Mall),
P.O.B. 1008 - Station B,
OTTAWA, Ont. KlP 5R1.
Tel. (613)238.8985-6
Toll Free: 1-800.267.4164
Librairie Renouf Limitée
980 rue Notre-Dame,
Lachine, P.Q. H8S 2B9,
Tel. (514) 634-7088.

DENMARK – DANEMARK
Munksgaard Export and Subscription Service
35, Nørre Søgade
DK 1370 KØBENHAVN K. Tel. +45.1.12.85.70

FINLAND – FINLANDE
Akateeminen Kirjakauppa
Keskuskatu 1, 00100 HELSINKI 10. Tel. 65.11.22

FRANCE
Bureau des Publications de l'OCDE,
2 rue André-Pascal, 75775 PARIS CEDEX 16. Tel. (1) 524.81.67
Principal correspondant :
13602 AIX-EN-PROVENCE : Librairie de l'Université.
Tel. 26.18.08

GERMANY – ALLEMAGNE
OECD Publications and Information Center
4 Simrockstrasse 5300 BONN N. Tel. (0228) 21.60.45

GREECE – GRÈCE
Librairie Kauffmann, 28 rue du Stade,
ATHÈNES 132. Tel. 322.21.60

HONG-KONG
Government Information Services,
Publications/Sales Section, Baskerville House,
2nd Floor, 22 Ice House Street

ICELAND – ISLANDE
Snaebjörn Jónsson and Co., h.f.,
Hafnarstraeti 4 and 9, P.O.B. 1131, REYKJAVIK.
Tel. 13133/14281/11936

INDIA – INDE
Oxford Book and Stationery Co. :
NEW DELHI-1, Scindia House. Tel. 45896
CALCUTTA 700016, 17 Park Street. Tel. 240832

INDONESIA – INDONÉSIE
PDIN-LIPI, P.O. Box 3065/JKT., JAKARTA, Tel. 583467

IRELAND – IRLANDE
TDC Publishers – Library Suppliers
12 North Frederick Street, DUBLIN 1 Tel. 744835-749677

ITALY – ITALIE
Libreria Commissionaria Sansoni :
Via Lamarmora 45, 50121 FIRENZE. Tel. 579751/584468
Via Bartolini 29, 20155 MILANO. Tel. 365083
Sub-depositari :
Ugo Tassi
Via A. Farnese 28, 00192 ROMA. Tel. 310590
Editrice e Libreria Herder,
Piazza Montecitorio 120, 00186 ROMA. Tel. 6794628
Costantino Ercolano, Via Generale Orsini 46, 80132 NAPOLI. Tel. 405210
Libreria Hoepli, Via Hoepli 5, 20121 MILANO. Tel. 865446
Libreria Scientifica, Dott. Lucio de Biasio "Aeiou"
Via Meravigli 16, 20123 MILANO Tel. 807679
Libreria Zanichelli
Piazza Galvani 1/A, 40124 Bologna Tel. 237389
Libreria Lattes, Via Garibaldi 3, 10122 TORINO. Tel. 519274
La diffusione delle edizioni OCSE è inoltre assicurata dalle migliori librerie nelle
città più importanti.

JAPAN – JAPON
OECD Publications and Information Center,
Landic Akasaka Bldg., 2-3-4 Akasaka,
Minato-ku, TOKYO 107 Tel. 586.2016

KOREA – CORÉE
Pan Korea Book Corporation,
P.O. Box n° 101 Kwangwhamun, SÉOUL. Tel. 72.7369

LEBANON – LIBAN
Documenta Scientifica/Redico,
Edison Building, Bliss Street, P.O. Box 5641, BEIRUT.
Tel. 354429 – 344425

MALAYSIA – MALAISIE
University of Malaya Co-operative Bookshop Ltd.
P.O. Box 1127, Jalan Pantai Baru
KUALA LUMPUR. Tel. 577701/577072

THE NETHERLANDS – PAYS-BAS
Staatsuitgeverij, Verzendboekhandel,
Chr. Plantijnstraat 1 Postbus 20014
2500 EA S-GRAVENHAGE. Tel. nr. 070.789911
Voor bestellingen: Tel. 070.789208

NEW ZEALAND – NOUVELLE-ZÉLANDE
Publications Section,
Government Printing Office Bookshops:
AUCKLAND: Retail Bookshop: 25 Rutland Street,
Mail Orders: 85 Beach Road, Private Bag C.P.O.
HAMILTON: Retail: Ward Street,
Mail Orders, P.O. Box 857
WELLINGTON: Retail: Mulgrave Street (Head Office),
Cubacade World Trade Centre
Mail Orders: Private Bag
CHRISTCHURCH: Retail: 159 Hereford Street,
Mail Orders: Private Bag
DUNEDIN: Retail: Princes Street
Mail Order: P.O. Box 1104

NORWAY – NORVÈGE
J.G. TANUM A/S
P.O. Box 1177 Sentrum OSLO 1. Tel. (02) 80.12.60

PAKISTAN
Mirza Book Agency, 65 Shahrah Quaid-E-Azam, LAHORE 3.
Tel. 66839

PORTUGAL
Livraria Portugal, Rua do Carmo 70-74,
1117 LISBOA CODEX. Tel. 360582/3

SINGAPORE – SINGAPOUR
Information Publications Pte Ltd,
Pei-Fu Industrial Building,
24 New Industrial Road N° 02-06
SINGAPORE 1953, Tel. 2831786, 2831798

SPAIN – ESPAGNE
Mundi-Prensa Libros, S.A.
Castelló 37, Apartado 1223, MADRID-1. Tel. 275.46.55
Libreria Bosch, Ronda Universidad 11, BARCELONA 7.
Tel. 317.53.08, 317.53.58

SWEDEN – SUÈDE
AB CE Fritzes Kungl Hovbokhandel,
Box 16 356, S 103 27 STH, Regeringsgatan 12,
DS STOCKHOLM. Tel. 08/23.89.00
Subscription Agency/Abonnements:
Wennergren-Williams AB,
Box 13004, S104 25 STOCKHOLM.
Tel. 08/54.12.00

SWITZERLAND – SUISSE
OECD Publications and Information Center
4 Simrockstrasse 5300 BONN (Germany). Tel. (0228) 21.60.45
Local Agents/Agents locaux
Librairie Payot, 6 rue Grenus, 1211 GENÈVE 11. Tel. 022.31.89.50

TAIWAN – FORMOSE
Good Faith Worldwide Int'l Co., Ltd.
9th floor, No. 118, Sec. 2,
Chung Hsiao E. Road
TAIPEI. Tel. 391.7396/391.7397

THAILAND – THAILANDE
Suksit Siam Co., Ltd., 1715 Rama IV Rd,
Samyan, BANGKOK 5. Tel. 2511630

TURKEY – TURQUIE
Kültur Yayinlari Is-Türk Ltd. Sti.
Atatürk Bulvari No : 191/Kat. 21
Kavaklidere/ANKARA. Tel. 17 02 66
Dolmabahce Cad. No : 29
BESIKTAS/ISTANBUL. Tel. 60 71 88

UNITED KINGDOM – ROYAUME-UNI
H.M. Stationery Office,
P.O.B 276, LONDON SW8 5DT.
(postal orders only)
Telephone orders: (01) 622.3316, or
49 High Holborn, LONDON WC1V 6 HB (personal callers)
Branches at: EDINBURGH, BIRMINGHAM, BRISTOL,
MANCHESTER, BELFAST.

UNITED STATES OF AMERICA – ÉTATS-UNIS
OECD Publications and Information Center, Suite 1207,
1750 Pennsylvania Ave., N.W. WASHINGTON, D.C.20006 – 4582
Tel. (202) 724.1857

VENEZUELA
Libreria del Este, Avda. F. Miranda 52, Edificio Galipan,
CARACAS 106. Tel. 32.23.01/33.26.04/31.58.38

YUGOSLAVIA – YOUGOSLAVIE
Jugoslovenska Knjiga, Knez Mihajlova 2, P.O.B. 36, BEOGRAD.
Tel. 621.992

Les commandes provenant de pays où l'OCDE n'a pas encore désigné de dépositaire peuvent être adressées à :
OCDE, Bureau des Publications, 2, rue André-Pascal, 75775 PARIS CEDEX 16.

Orders and inquiries from countries where sales agents have not yet been appointed may be sent to:
OECD, Publications Office, 2, rue André-Pascal, 75775 PARIS CEDEX 16.

68236-12-1984

OECD PUBLICATIONS
2, rue André-Pascal
75775 PARIS CEDEX 16
No. 43149
(10 85 11 1) ISBN 92-64-12680-5
ISSN 0376-6438

●

PRINTED IN FRANCE